HEROES ALL

My 2006 Ryder Cup Story

HEROES ALL

My 2006 Ryder Cup Story

Darren Clarke

HODDER &
STOUGHTON

First published in Great Britain in 2006 by Hodder & Stoughton
A division of Hodder Headline

The right of Darren Clarke to be identified as the Author of the Work has been
asserted by him in accordance with the Copyright, Designs and Patents Act 1988.

A Hodder and Stoughton Book

1

A CIP catalogue record for this title is available from the British Library

ISBN 978 0 340 937167
ISBN 0 340 937165

Typeset in Stempel Garamond by Hewer Text UK Ltd, Edinburgh

Printed and bound by
Clays Ltd, St Ives plc

Hodder Headline's policy is to use papers that are natural, renewable and
recyclable products and made from wood grown in sustainable forests.
The logging and manufacturing processes are expected to conform to the
environmental regulations of the country of origin.

Hodder & Stoughton Ltd
A division of Hodder Headline
338 Euston Road
London NW1 3BH

To Heather

Contents

Acknowledgements

This book would not have been possible without many people, who know who they are, but are too numerous to mention.

It would be unfair, however, not to single out one or two, primarily my parents, Godfrey and Hetty, Heather's mum, Anne, and my boys, Tyrone and Conor, for letting me go and play.

I have been indebted all my career to the guidance I have received from my manager, Andrew 'Chubby' Chandler, managing director of International Sports Management. His unwavering support throughout everything has shown him to be what he is, a true friend.

This book being mainly about the Ryder Cup, it would be remiss not to mention Europe's captain, Ian Woosnam, for having the courage to pick me; also Woosie's wife Glendryth, all my wonderful team-mates and their partners, American captain, Tom Lehman, and his wife Melissa and the US team and their partners, for their encouragement and support throughout the week. I will not forget how good they all were to me.

The European players will forgive me for giving special mention to Lee John Westwood for being Lee John and to Paul and Alison McGinley, who have gone through so much with me and were such great friends of Heather and so good to the boys.

This tome would not be on the shelves now, but for the foresight and enthusiasm of the indefatigable Roddy Bloomfield of Hodder, who has published more than 1,000 books in his career and shows no signs of slowing down.

Finally, my thanks to Martin Hardy for helping and directing me through everything media-related since Heather passed away. He also arranged my words for this book into some kind of order, together with his Ryder Cup team, Andrew Farrell, Suzanne de la Perrelle, Claudia Kalindjian and Nicolas Kidd.

My sincere thanks to you all.

Photographic acknowledgements

The author and publisher would like to thank the following for permission to reproduce photographs:

Action Images, AFP/Getty Images, AP/Empics, Empics, Getty Images, PA/Empics.

Preface

When I made myself available – if required – for the 2006 Ryder Cup, I knew that the first hole I played would amount to the toughest thing I had ever encountered in golf or was ever likely to. I was not wrong.

From the moment Captain Ian Woosnam told me to get my spikes ready, the 1st tee on the Friday morning was at the forefront of my thoughts. I'm not going to say precisely how I was feeling for fear of sounding like a 36-handicapper, but let's say I wasn't particularly looking forward to it and had absolutely no idea in what direction the ball would fly off the clubface. If anything, I'd underestimated exactly what would be waiting for me, even though a million things were going through my mind.

The fact that I had partner Lee Westwood there as my crutch made it an awful lot easier, not that it was in any way, shape or form, easy. But with a good friend by my side, and one who knew me inside out, it was definitely easier.

I knew I had to stand up and be counted. I had to do it. I had to get through it . . . and I would.

Help also came from the most unlikely of quarters. I'd seen my good friend Tiger Woods not hit the shot he wanted off the 1st tee and finish in the water. It was reassuring to know that even the best player in the world could do such a thing because I thought, 'What's the worst thing that can happen to you?'

How I hit the ball, I am not quite sure, but I absolutely flushed it straight down the middle, almost holed the approach and when I saw the 15-foot putt that I had left, I just knew, was absolutely certain, that I was going to hole it. I had never been more certain of anything in my life. And so it came to pass, or drop, in this particular case.

I am also sure that Heather was with me the entire week. She was looking over me on the 1st tee, on the first green. I'm convinced she was there – just watching out for me, as she always did.

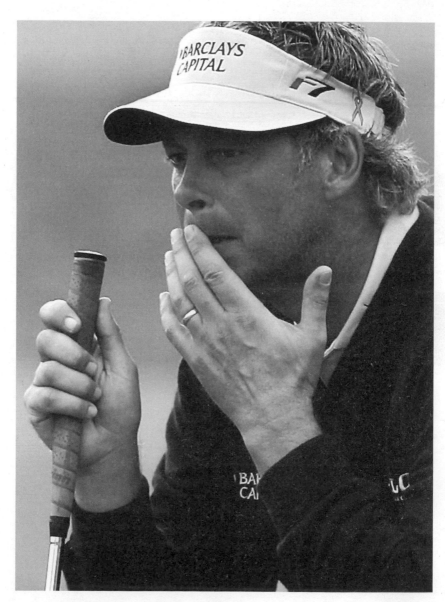

It was back to work at the Madrid Open.

1 | WILD CARD

I decided to stop playing golf after my last round of the 2006 Open Championship at Hoylake. It was not a difficult decision. It had taken a really big effort for me to play the European Open at the K Club, even bigger for the Barclays Scottish Open at Loch Lomond, and I was really only at the Open because it was the Open, my favourite tournament of the year.

My mind really wasn't on golf all that often. In fact, it wasn't on much else apart from my wife Heather and our two boys, Tyrone, eight, and Conor, five – the heartbeats of my life. I'd committed myself to these three tournaments, but my mind was made up that I would play no more for the foreseeable future after Hoylake. Four years of the bravest and most courageous battle against that dreadful disease cancer were beginning to take their toll. It was obvious that Heather was going downhill fast.

It had not been easy playing for a while. When I did not play well, it was because I could not concentrate and even when I did string a series of decent shots together and worked my way into contention, I had the utmost problem preventing my mind from straying and consequently never completed the job. When the finishing line is in sight, it is imperative for a golfer to concentrate on nothing other than crossing it, but as the golfing summer reached its zenith there were too many mental hurdles in my way and I'd invariably blow my chances. My mind would be elsewhere and that's fatal in golf, as it proved at Loch Lomond, where I so wanted to win for my sponsors, Barclays. I led going into the last round, had a great chance to succeed, but just could not do it, posting a 72 – the highest score of anybody who finished in the top twenty – to slump to a very disappointing joint fifth. I don't enter tournaments to do that.

I would normally look forward to Open week with keen anticipation and excitement and this one was particularly attractive because world golf's biggest championship had not been played at Hoylake, a wonderful links on the Wirral, for thirty-nine years – longer than I have been alive. Sadly, I just could not raise too much enthusiasm and although the start was encouraging, a 69, the finish was much less so. I could not find any spark. I hate having to admit it, but there was simply no fight in me and that's not me. I slumped to an 82. There was no consolation that it was not the worst round of the day.

My Open was over after two rounds, not surprising since my mind was constantly wandering off back down the M6 to home and the stark reality of what was waiting. After fighting every inch of the way through countless sessions of chemotherapy and the false dawns of occasional remission, Heather's life was now a struggle. She had been the one kicking me out the door to play, but now I needed to be with her and the boys and not on the golf course.

The Ryder Cup was of no relevance whatsoever to me at that stage. It was too far in the future to think about and I had more pressing things to occupy my thoughts, living a day at a time with Heather. As it transpired, she deteriorated very rapidly, which was horrible both to witness and be part of, not to mention heart-breaking. Her secondary breast cancer was always going to lead to the day that was fast approaching.

After Heather passed away, and a few days of basically feeling numb, it was a case of trying to get my thoughts and act together to see what was possible and what was not. After a week of soul-searching, I had to decide if I would be up for the challenge of the Ryder Cup.

The days passed by and with the realisation that I would have to make some kind of decision before it was too late, I finally came to the conclusion that I had to do it because that's exactly what Heather would have wanted me to do. It was not an easy decision, but no matter how many times I debated it in my mind, I always came to the same ending – Heather would want me to.

I decided to make myself available, but only after I had convinced myself that I would be of benefit to the team. If I was going to play, then I was going to have to contribute, because the Ryder Cup is no place for passengers. Can I win matches? Can I get through the week? Can I cope with the spotlight, emotion and pressure? It was only when I could answer 'yes' to all those questions that I made it known that I was up for the Cup.

It was a combination of desire and knowledge that convinced me I would be of use to Europe. Ian Woosnam, a wonderful and fiercely determined golfer, spoke to me about a week after Heather passed away, although our conversation did not stray much from him passing on his condolences and asking how I was doing. That was all. There was no real mention of the Ryder Cup, but I told him I'd been thinking about it a lot and if he wanted me to play then I would. I also told him that although I wanted to be a wild card, I would not go wild if he did not pick me. I would have no issues with him whatsoever. Woosie was understanding, but noncommittal.

A couple of weeks later, on the Friday of the BMW International in Munich and two days before the team would be announced, Woosie called me again and told me to get my spikes ready.

I was delighted that he had decided to make me one of his picks because I had put an awful lot of work into trying to get my game into shape in the previous three weeks. My coach Ewen Murray, former Tour player turned Sky golf commentator, joined me on the range at home as bucket after bucket of balls was emptied. I had known that there was no guarantee that I was going to be picked, but I just wanted to make sure that, if the call came, I was ready. When the phone rang, I knew that I was.

It would be my fifth Ryder Cup and the first time I had been picked. It was good to know that Woosie held me in high enough regard to give me one of the two places that were available to the captain. I had no idea whom he had in mind for the other spot, but all the talk in the papers was that it looked like being between Thomas Bjorn and Lee Westwood, both great players. Thomas had had a better season but Lee is a magnificent Ryder Cup player who had twice won at the K Club. These were two of my best friends on the Tour and I felt slightly awkward at being in the middle.

To be honest, I really felt for Thomas when he didn't get the nod. The Dane, as I call him, always wears his heart on his sleeve and he's a fabulous player who had done everything he could to make the team. We all want to be part of it and Thomas has seen both sides, having been a player twice, both times in winning teams, and as an assistant to Bernhard Langer in Detroit, scene of Europe's record triumph.

Thomas knows exactly what it's like to sample the elation of winning and how good it tastes and was desperate to be part of it again. It was obviously a very difficult time for him when his name was not one of the two to be added to the ten who had automatically qualified.

There are times when Thomas sometimes speaks from his heart before actually thinking about what might come out of his mouth. That's not meant as criticism because I do exactly the same thing at times. Thomas is brutally honest and that's why I think the world of him. He's one of my best friends and always will be, and I like the fact that he calls a spade a spade. As with me, on occasions, diplomacy is not one of his virtues and that's part of the reason I get on so well with him.

Thomas was hurting in Munich and he let rip, although he probably looks back now and wishes he'd taken a couple of things out of his rant, but I could not really fault the guy in general for what he said. If he had left out a couple of personal things about Woosie, I don't think anybody would have had an issue with him and, with the advantage of hindsight, I'm sure he realises that.

I was right in the middle of it because Lee and I are very, very close pals who travel the world, practise and dine and drink together. It was not my decision and I had nothing to do with it. On the one hand, I was bitterly disappointed for Thomas, but on the other I was absolutely delighted for Lee. He'd been through a tough spell, but he came good when he had to. Also, our record together in the Ryder Cup is reasonably good and we enjoy one another's company.

Woosie's position was terrible. Picking two players can be just so difficult and definitely one of the hardest things that a captain has to do, arguably *the* hardest. It's not going to get any easier for Woosie's successors because the way Europe is producing players at the moment, captains are going to have more and more world-class options to select from. Maybe there is a case for just going down the world rankings and then nobody can argue.

It was a tough call but, as was subsequently shown with the results board at the Ryder Cup on the Sunday, you cannot argue against anything that Woosie did before or during. He was simply a great captain.

Having got the nod from Woosie, I couldn't come back to play in the Ryder Cup without teeing up in a tournament beforehand. It would have been impossible and irresponsible even to have considered it. It just wasn't feasible. The only one I could play was in Madrid. Actually, that's not quite accurate because I did play in another event – the 2006 Queenwood Club Championship, which I was defending, and now I have my name on the honours board twice at my home club because I managed to bring the trophy back with me again.

A lot of the media noticed before the wild cards were chosen that the closing date for entry into the Madrid event came during the BMW in Germany. I had entered before I knew I had a pick, but some of the media put two and two together and got five again. I had entered in the hope of getting a pick, not in the knowledge, but a lot of people decided that I already knew. I didn't. If Woosie didn't pick me, I still had time to withdraw from Madrid and play the American Express at the Grove, which is what I would have done.

The way I looked at it was that if I did get a pick, I would play in Madrid, but I had to enter first, so that's what happened and a group of us jetted off to sunny Spain in the Challenger, the private aeroplane that I share with Lee Westwood. With me were my right-hand man John Newton, a former Miss World bodyguard, and Martin Hardy, ISM's media consultant, who was to orchestrate my first public appearance since Heather's passing away. The ordeal was every bit as trying as I had expected, but it had to be faced.

One of the toughest things I have ever had to do was face the media that week because questioning about Heather, the boys and my situation was always going to be central to anything else the journalists may have wanted to ask. There are not many things that make me apprehensive, but this was one, no matter that I had faced the men from Fleet Street, Ireland and the rest of the world hundreds of times before. I knew most of those who crammed into the flimsy marquee that served as a press centre at La Moraleja on the outskirts of the Spanish capital

After thinking about it and talking it over with those closest to me, I had decided that the best way to get it all over and done with in one hit was to go into the media centre and let them ask anything and everything for as long as they wanted. They had not seen me since Heather passed away, so they were bound to ask some very difficult questions that would test my emotions.

As soon as I finished my pro-am round with three Spaniards, who spoke little English, I was ready to face my interrogators. The subject of Heather soon came up, as expected.

How hard a decision had it been letting Ian Woosnam know I was available if needed? I admitted that it had been pretty tough, but insisted that I wouldn't have volunteered had I not thought that I could benefit the team. That had been the bottom line because I knew that Heather would have wanted me to play. 'Heather would not have wanted me to sit about moping at home. She would have wanted me to get back out working again,' I said.

Was there anything in my mind saying that it might be too soon to return to playing? Not really because Heather had been diagnosed two weeks after the last Ryder Cup, so her cancer was not something that had happened out of the blue. I knew what was going to happen, as most people in similar circumstances do. I had made the decision and would always feel that it was the right one for everybody concerned.

It had been important from a golfing point of view that the format was matchplay because if I had carded a 10 anywhere, it would not have made much difference to the overall scheme of things. It was one on one or two on two and did not have the same intensity as strokeplay.

I told them that the most difficult thing for me was my boys being still quite young. Dealing with them more closely on a day-to-day basis was something that I had to get used to and would do as a single parent, but I had been thankful for all the support I had had from both my and Heather's family and friends.

It seemed a strange question, but somebody asked if I had found inner calm. I had found a lot of things, but I was not sure if that was one of them, and those closest to me would testify that the adjective is not one that would be among the first used to describe me.

'Things are massively different from what they were before, and at some stage I have had to grow up, and this is the perfect time for it.' I added, 'I have extra responsibilities now and I have to do the right thing, both for my boys and myself. I have to pay the bills because nobody else will do that for me, but I've talked a lot to Tyrone and Conor at home and explained everything that's going on. Even though they're only eight and five, they sort of grasp what I'm doing. Every decision I've made so far, I've sat down and talked to them about it, to explain what's going on.'

Somebody wondered what it would be that got me through what was bound to be an emotionally charged atmosphere and I came back very quickly.

'I will get myself through it. Nobody else,' I said. 'My team and everybody else will help with support, but I will deal with it and I will get through it and enjoy the week.'

No matter how often the talk shifted from my personal life, somebody would invariably bring it back. Sometimes I wonder if the people asking those questions could imagine sitting up where I was and how they might react. If there was a little role reversal, things might be rather different. Unfortunately, that's not the way it is. I'm a professional golfer and people are entitled to ask their questions, but sometimes it would be nice if people thought before they asked.

Did I have any sense of dread about the emotional aspect at the Ryder Cup? I said dread was too strong a word, but I would be a liar if I said there wouldn't be a few times when I would probably feel uncomfortable. 'It was always coming at some stage that I would have to stand up and get on with my life and this is what I'm trying to do,' I said.

It ended with a question about whether I felt stronger for what had happened. 'I have battled through a lot of things that a lot of people never have to,' I said. 'I have had to face up to a lot of tough things and I feel I have come out of it a better person. I hope I have.'

I had come through the questioning with just one difficult moment early into the interview when my voice betrayed my emotions and I had to compose myself and drink some water. But I got through it against the cream of Fleet Street and Irish golf writing, along with a couple of probing television lenses.

After throttling back on those early tears, I had continued without a further blip. It was another of my tiny steps, trying to do the best I could in whatever circumstances I found myself in.

I answered all the questions and all that was left for the media to discover was whether I could still swing a club. I had no doubt that I had not lost my game in the mists of uncertainty and time, but I was particularly nervous and worried in the first round because I did so want to shoot a decent score. If I'd rattled up a 75, people would have been on my case and questioning my selection.

Fortunately, I played very nicely and shot 68. I sent Woosie a text, saying, 'I bet you're as happy about that as I am.' That was it. I was off again, fine. I didn't finish the week as well as I would have liked to have done, but my game was in decent shape and I knew it. I'd tested it first at the K Club on the Thursday before Madrid.

I took the plane over with Woosie and a few of the other team members, played, stayed the night and flew home.

Now I was ready for the big stage again, and they come no bigger than the Ryder Cup. I was also looking forward to a proper drop of the black stuff. Guinness tastes no better than when consumed in its Dublin home.

Ian Woosnam welcomes Tom Lehman at Dublin Airport.

2 | MONDAY, 18 September

It was a week I had to get through, would get through, on my own, so perhaps it was fitting that I was the only passenger on board the Challenger I share with my very good friend Lee John Westwood when it took off on Monday morning, 18 September, from Farnborough. We headed to Dublin via Doncaster where I collected my fourball partner and his wife Laurae.

We had already cleared it to fly separately, rather than in the team jet from Heathrow. Captain Woosnam was okay with this because Jose Maria Olazabal and Sergio Garcia were coming in from Spain independently in their jets so, as it was a home game, it was deemed all right for us to travel as we wanted. It meant I didn't have to go through Heathrow where there may have been more media focus than I wanted to attract. I was determined that I should be accepted as one member of the team, not as an object for individual attention and sympathy because I had lost my wife just a few weeks earlier. That's what I wanted. Some hope . . . to some extent understandably.

The three of us flew to Dublin in the Challenger and when we arrived it was pouring with rain. Chema, as Jose Maria is known by family and friends, arrived next. He was leaving his plane and heading for the VIP area when we ambushed him and brought him on board with us for a beer. Then Sergio's plane arrived, so we went to find him and invited him to the impromptu party as well, which meant there were five of us sharing a little aperitif while we waited for the rest of the boys to arrive from Heathrow on the Aer Lingus charter.

We were eventually taken out to greet the others, posed for pictures, waved and pressed the flesh, but we were quickly on to a coach and on our way to the K Club without too much hassle. Fortunately, we had Garda outriders, which made the trip very easy and much quicker than it would have been normally. It took us thirty minutes for a journey that has been known to take some people through several shaving zones. Woosie and Glendryth were on the bus with us and we went straight into the hotel at the K Club and up to our rooms. They had billeted us in a slightly different part of the hotel from where I normally stay. The Americans were on the first floor and we were on the second, which was not a situation I hoped would be mirrored in the following Sunday's standings . . . although I did want us to remain on top, obviously.

One of the many beauties of the Ryder Cup is that when you walk into your room your clothes for the week are already waiting for you. On the rail were the team uniforms for every single practice day, the match days and official functions. It is at that point that the first real buzz of the week arrives. When you see the uniforms all ready, game time isn't far away.

Qualification had started more than a year previously, but for the twelve good enough and lucky enough to make the team, this is the moment when any doubt about what the week is all about disappears. You want the Ryder Cup to start then and there, but there are still three more full days to go – an eternity to the impetuous –

before team golf's greatest competition unfolds before an expectant nation and a worldwide television audience of one billion people.

It is said that the Ryder Cup is now the third biggest event in global sport behind the World Cup and the Olympics, which says much for what Jack Nicklaus, Tony Jacklin and others helped do for the competition. At one stage, it was not of much interest even to those who played in it, and was watched by scarcely more people than were inside the ropes.

It used to be that the Americans turned up and won, but since Nicklaus encouraged Great Britain and Ireland to widen eligibility to include Europe, gradually the balance of power has swung the other way.

Something else has changed. In the days of Europe's big five, Seve Ballesteros, Nick Faldo, Bernhard Langer, Sandy Lyle and Ian Woosnam, the European team was top heavy, but in recent contests there has been a spread of quality across the board. When I looked at our team it was virtually impossible to put it in any kind of order apart from seniority. Chema has won a couple of Majors and Colin Montgomerie has a magnificent Ryder Cup and Order of Merit record, but we had arrived at the K Club in County Kildare with twelve proper players . . . and, as they would prove, heroes all. It's not for me to say whether this was Europe's greatest team of all time, but as American captain Tom Lehman pointed out afterwards, 'I doubt that any team has ever played better.'

Back in my room, the only difference from previous Ryder Cups was that there were no women's clothes on the rail. Even as she entered the closing stages of her courageous fight, Heather had been concerned about whether her outfits for the week she so loved would be ready in time. She never got to wear them and, even though I inspected mine closely, the significance of the pink jackets for the closing ceremony was lost on me until the event itself. It was one of many moving touches throughout the week.

With clothes all taken care of ahead of arrival, it is always a case of travelling light during Ryder Cup week. All we need to bring are a couple of pairs of jeans and a few shirts. It took me a few minutes to unpack my stuff and then it was down into the team room.

The minute we all got there the atmosphere was fantastic. There was instant camaraderie. I hadn't seen a few of the guys and their partners since Heather passed away and they all had hugs and kind words for me. Meeting my team-mates and just getting into the style of things was quite settling, but I would not have been there at all had I not thought I could carry it off, on the course particularly, but also off it. Nevertheless, it was nice to feel the genuine warmth and kindness of everybody around me.

We were now into the week and I had two options. Either I crumbled like a cheap deck of cards or got on with things. I quickly decided that if I was into crumble it was just the apple variety. Whatever else happened, I was going to get through the week – having put myself forward for selection, I owed it to my captain and team-mates, family and friends, and not least myself. I was going to get on with things, and that's exactly what I did.

The team room was a very relaxing place to be. The jukebox had about 10,000 songs on it and something for everybody, but the favoured record of the week seemed to be by the Scissor Sisters.

At the first team meeting of the week, Woosie told me that I would be partnered with Lee in practice. It was a relief because that was what

I wanted to hear, even though I was prepared to play with anybody. My relationship with Lee has been built over a long time and on every one of the golf-playing continents. We have mutual respect because we have been trying to beat one another for so long, and we have had such great times together in previous Ryder Cups that this was always going to be another good one. Lee is a very easy guy to play with. He is a strong influence on me, and probably knows better than most how to control my occasional tantrums and eccentricities. We have travelled the world together, practised together, partnered one another and know one another's game inside out.

We also knew the K Club very well – Lee having won twice there and me having shot one of my two 60s there, although the course had been considerably toughened since that memorable day in the last century. I did feel that home advantage might be more significant than usual because we had played several tournaments on the course. We were familiar with how things changed in varying conditions, and how certain holes would play differently from normal in tough weather. It might not prove a huge advantage, but even a small advantage could be crucial in a tight match.

With the course lengthened, greens changed and trees growing, it was a much more difficult course than the one where I shot 60 during the Smurfit European Open of 1999. It wasn't an easy course then, but probably two or three shots easier than the Arnold Palmer course that confronted us now.

However, this was matchplay, and in this form of the game you can afford to take on a few things that you wouldn't normally do in strokeplay. It is more a question of knowing when the time is right or wrong to go for something. You definitely have to mix things up in matchplay and decide whether to go for the flag or hit into the fat of the green. Sometimes you pay the penalty for being a little too aggressive and sometimes the reward is worth the risk. That's the beauty of the game.

We didn't know whether Woosie was intending to use Lee and me in fourballs or foursomes or both, and I didn't ask. I was there because he wanted me to be there and I was happy to go along with playing in whatever capacity he chose. Had he played me just once or asked me to go out six times (I know the maximum is five) it would not have bothered me. Woosie said he was pairing us with Padraig and Paul for the following morning, which would make for an interesting match . . . and hopefully some easy money and bragging rights. I always view practice rounds as the chance not only to see the course but to find out how your opponents cope when they are playing for their own money. We have a lot of fun and banter during these games, but some are not easily parted from their money.

There were other off-course commitments to attend to before we could start our practice in earnest. Not least was the mandatory press conference where a bank of cameras from all parts of the world were trained on me, the operators no doubt hoping that I would show a hint of weakness and choke whenever the questioning, as it invariably would, got round to Heather. I knew I would disappoint them because, although it was something of an ordeal facing many more than a hundred hard-nosed hacks, I had survived a much more daunting examination the previous week in Madrid. Far fewer people had been in attendance, but it was the first time I'd bared my soul to the media and the first time is the worst.

At the K Club, I was relaxed, in control of my emotions and

ready for whatever might be thrown at me. I was never going to dodge any questions, but it was nice to be the first of the players to get in there, and not have to worry about it for the rest of the week. I was able to confront things head on and just tell them how I was thinking and feeling. I did not want to leave anything to doubt or offer room for invention.

It did not take long for the *Irish Examiner*'s Charlie Mulqueen, whom I have known for many years, to pose the question that got pens poised and prompted close-in focus from the television cameras. Would I expect it to be an emotional occasion on the 1st tee on Friday? I parried it, to much laughter, by asking Charlie if he knew something I didn't – that I would actually be playing on Friday.

The laughter broke the ice and I was able to tell the gathering that there were bound to be difficult moments, but the 1st tee would not be one of them because that would be back to golfing things, and golf is what I do.

I said that I would not be more nervous than I had been in previous Ryder Cups and, although the emotional side would play a factor somewhere along the line, when the golf started, it was back to business for me.

Charlie would not drop the bone and asked if I'd feel happier on the course than off it. Truthfully, I was not bad in other places, but overall I was comfortable with what I was doing. I had thought long and hard about whether I should or shouldn't be there and had come to the conclusion that I would help and benefit the team if I was. 'That's why I'm here,' I said. 'I want to play. I want to compete and I want to help my team-mates.'

Another questioner kept on the emotional theme with even greater intensity and little sensitivity, but I stressed that my purpose in being there was to play golf and help the team – otherwise I wouldn't have come.

Respite came when the questioning turned to how big a deal it was for Ireland to host the Ryder Cup and I told them how desperate I had been to be part of what was going to be a magnificent and unbelievable occasion for the country. There was also the question of bonding with players you are normally trying to beat week in, week out, and the feelings of respect that would endure for a long time.

But it did not take long for the inquisition to return to those who would not be there. Tiger had lost his father and Chris DiMarco his mum, so the Ryder Cup was not life and death. There were more important things than trying to win, but we were all professionals and wanted to win for our teams. As friendly as we were with the Americans, we would want to kick their butts as much as they would want to redden ours.

Tom Lehman had said that the Ryder Cup would be better for me being in it and Tiger had also publicly lent his support, as had the players and officials of both sides, so it was gratifying to know people were behind me.

The press were on a roll now and determined to eke out every last detail of my off-course predicament. As horrible as it had been, had any good come out of it? To that I replied that it had brought me closer to my boys and I'd had to look after them more than I would normally have done. If there was any positive, that was the only thing, because it had been difficult watching Heather suffer for four years.

In general, I think the press conference went well. I answered all the questions and tried to do what I thought I should be doing and say honestly what I wanted to.

One particular area was not covered. There had been doubt in some quarters about whether I should or should not have been in the team and I respect that people are entitled to their opinions, but once Woosie offered me a spot I made my decision to play and I stood by it.

An Irish newspaper had conducted a poll on whether or not it was right that I should play and opinion appeared to be divided. The point those who thought I should not play – because I had not grieved for long enough – seemed to have missed was that, actually, I had been grieving for two years and not just since Heather had passed away. When the cancer came back it was a very, very sad time for us. We had thought that she was doing okay after her previous operations. We believed that she had battled through and the worst was over. Unfortunately, that was not the case and it came back with a vengeance. We knew from that day that it was a time issue in terms of life expectancy. There would be no full remission. That's when the grieving started.

Heather did go into remission a few times after her cancer returned, but they were still difficult times because she was going backward and forward to hospital for checks and tests. I had been trying to prepare myself and, although you can never be totally ready, it wasn't as if she had died in a car crash.

We had known that it was a question of when not if, and eventually the doctors got to the situation where they had done everything they possibly could and could do no more. We flew to

America as a last resort, but because Heather had had treatment previously for a heart problem that had nearly killed her, her heart was just not strong enough to try a new drug on a trial basis.

It was a case of returning home and letting nature take its course. Heather passed away peacefully in her sleep at the Royal Marsden Hospital in the early hours of Sunday, 13 August. Never once throughout her courageous battle, even when life was slipping away, did she complain of her lot. She was one brave lady.

Those people who took it upon themselves to decide it was too soon for me to come back, or even suggest it, were merely offering a personal opinion. The only person who knows what can or cannot be done in the circumstances is you yourself. An outsider's judgment is a very tough call indeed. People who have been in the same position as me, as far as I'm aware, all seem to react differently.

Heather would have wanted me to play and I knew that if I felt I could do it, and play as well as I could, I would be doing it as much for her as for myself. That knowledge gave me the impetus to perform the way that I did.

Having finished with the written media, radio and the majority of television, I was obliged to be interviewed by NBC and Sky, the two official networks, in their clubhouse studios. Both interviews were conducted very respectfully and Sky's Tim Barter, who has been a good friend over many years, was particularly mindful of not turning the interview into too personal an ordeal.

I told Tim to fire away and ask whatever he wanted and he eventually asked about Heather and the boys. I answered by telling him the way we were feeling – trying to get on with things and get some order into our lives. The boys had been fantastic and, although their mum had gone, I was trying to give them every possible bit of support I could, and was trying to make myself both mum and dad to them at the same time. Finally, he asked what made Darren Clarke tick and I replied simply and honestly, 'My boys and nothing else.'

It was a Kleenex moment because, although I was in control of myself, when I looked across at Barty, he had tears in his eyes. So I stopped the interview and said to him, 'Barty, it's supposed to be me that's crying, not you.' Bless him, he's a lovely guy and it was a little piece of black humour at a time when there had been so very little even to smile about.

Then it was back to the hotel and after a very relaxing dinner and a couple of pints of the black stuff – there were no restrictions on what we did, ate or drank unlike with some previous captains – we were entertained by Jamil Qureshi, a performance coach, who is no mean magician and mind-reader. We were also presented with inscribed Rolex watches as a present from the Tour. This was something of an embarrassing situation for Lee and me because we are both contracted to wear Audemars Piguet, from the luxury Swiss watch manufacturer, founded in 1875. It was a predicament we had faced before in Oakland Hills. So now I have two Rolex, which no doubt in time will find their way on to the wrists of Tyrone and Conor.

It was not much later than 10 p.m. when I retired to the loneliness of my room. Closing the door on the world and being home alone after lights out is something I have had to get accustomed to, but it has not got any easier as the days since Heather's passing add up.

Official practice gets under way at the K Club.

3 | TUESDAY, 19 September

Tuesday morning started bright and early, which was no hardship for me. I am invariably up and ready to go whenever I have to be. Lee and I took on Padraig and Paul for a few quid and we had an excellent game. The pair of us always have a lot of fun in practice and our etiquette is probably not what it would be in normal circumstances. We enjoy the banter and a few bets and we are a fairly formidable pair, which can be seen from the fact that nobody really likes playing against us – it normally involves losing money.

Lee and I were ahead and then Paul and Padraig started making a lot of birdies, which put them in a position of dormie two. I made 3 on the par 4 17th to get it back to one down, while Lee made 3 and an eagle on the 18th for us to square the match. We won money on the press and that did not go down too well with our opponents.

I think we were playing for a couple of hundred euros. It certainly wasn't enough anyway, but they wouldn't play for more. Obviously our reputation had gone ahead of us.

The crowds were out there for the first time in a practice round and they were simply fantastic. What on earth would it be like on Friday morning? We could only guess, but with just under three days to go we could sense already that this Ryder Cup was going to be like no other.

We hadn't seen anything of the Americans to date, but walking from the 9th green to the 10th tee during that practice session, I spotted Tiger on the range, hitting balls. What he'd said previously about me prompted me to go over to say thank you. We had that hug that was caught on camera and went round the world. It was a very special moment. His feelings showed what a genuine and fantastic person he is.

What Tiger said was for my ears only. He's a very private guy when it comes to that kind of thing and quite rightly so. We all should have our privacy when it comes to matters that are close to the heart but, because of the arena and era in which we work, we are expected to open our hearts a little bit too much at times. Let's just say that during his father's illness and Heather's we had some very heartfelt words for one another. What has happened has made us even closer friends than we were.

I'd seen Tiger at the Open at the stage when I knew things were not good for Heather and he'd not long been back after the death of his father. I was very moved when, at home in Surrey on the Sunday afternoon, I saw him breakdown on the 18th green after his triumph. I just can't explain how highly I regard him because he is the best player in the world and conducts himself in the best possible way he can all the time. He's just an unbelievable person.

After the match with Padraig and Paul and a bit of practice in the afternoon it was back to the hotel to prepare for the welcome dinner that night in the clubhouse at the K Club. We were all dressed in the finest Roberto Cavalli, which had been provided for us, and I sat beside Tiger throughout dinner, along with Tom and Melissa Lehman and Woosie and his wife Glen, JJ Henry and his wife.

It was the first time I had sat down with Tiger for as long as ninety minutes for a long time and we had a good old chat. I was very appreciative of his support, as I was of everybody else's. People were looking out for me and making sure I was all right because, although others did not have partners with them, my situation was different from theirs.

I was too busy talking to have a lot to eat, but everything was fine and I do know I downed a couple of pints of Guinness again. Then it was back to the team room to play the jukebox. I think I put on some modern dance music because when I'm at home in my den, which doubles as a gym and office, I always have MTV on. Even though I'm getting a little bit too old for that kind of stuff, I like to think I'm always up to date with what's going on and the latest fashions in clothes and music. Being in Ireland, a lot of U2 was also chosen. I think there was a table-tennis table downstairs, but the bar was upstairs, so that's where I ended up spending most of my leisure time.

Everybody mixed in well, including the two rookies – Henrik Stenson, a very strong player whose talent knows no boundaries, and Robert Karlsson, a quiet but quietly confident person who had come through the disappointment of having missed out on previous teams to qualify in style. They were the only two newcomers in our side, and they slotted in effortlessly, adding to the team's strength.

What a joyous place our team room was from start to finish. It would not have been the same without the Harringtons, Padraig, one of the world's best, and his bubbly wife, Caroline. Padraig had lost his father the previous year and knew everything that I was feeling, while Caroline was so supportive, both on the course and in the team room. I just could not imagine a Ryder Cup without either of them. The same goes for Monty, a natural-born leader and the one we all want at number one. Eight Ryder Cup singles without defeat speaks for itself.

I had noticed changes in others since the last match in Detroit. Luke Donald has a very funny side that is rarely seen in public, and from a playing point I am convinced he will continue going all the way up the world-rankings ladder until he reaches the top. Sergio is the heartbeat of the Ryder Cup team room and another legendary Spaniard in this competition, following on from Seve and Chema and all the others. He's simply a joy to be around and his enthusiasm is infectious. He's also a proper world-class player.

Jose Maria Olazabal is an out-and-out gentleman, who never gives up when facing the sternest of tasks – his long successful battle against a debilitating back condition is testimony to his courage. I couldn't have been happier for Paul McGinley, who was struggling for form coming into the match and played brilliantly all week

I was one of the elder statesmen of our side and so I said just a few words to the rookies about what it was going to be like on the 1st tee. I mentioned a few other little bits and pieces that I thought would help them and ensure that there were no surprises, but since the guys nowadays play a worldwide schedule, the days of being intimidated by anybody are long since gone. I told them how noisy it was going to be and how to determine which noises were for what side and so how to tell who had won a hole. They really didn't need to be told much, but it's always good to promote team spirit, although I wasn't the only one doing that.

Monty was very relaxed all week, with his arms round everybody, making sure things were going okay, while you could see the confidence surrounding Paul Casey, who had just come from winning the World Matchplay at Wentworth. He's turned into one of the best players in the world and he has that air about him. Then there was David Howell, Dangerous Dave, as we affectionately know him, chipping in with a few choice comments here and there that had everybody laughing.

Lee was waiting for anybody to drop a verbal *faux pas* so he could jump on him from a great height, as he invariably does. My great friend, travelling companion and practice and team partner is also an outstanding hypochondriac. One of the first things I have to do whenever we go anywhere together is find the nearest pharmacy. He's always sick and it normally ranges from about Tuesday 5 p.m. to Wednesday 10 a.m. and, strangely enough, then he's okay.

Our team room was a very relaxing place to be because, unlike previous Ryder Cups, when there had been three or four top players who had been expected to perform all week, this time we had twelve great players. Everybody was comfortable with what was going on and what awaited them when the match started. We were unbelievably confident and really looking forward to getting going. It was almost as if, without any disrespect to our opponents, we knew our destiny

There was just time for another pint of Guinness and then it was off to bed.

High winds cause the course to be closed early on Wednesday morning.

4 | WEDNESDAY, 20 September

Woosie's captaincy style was very laid-back. When he spoke to the entire team, which wasn't very often, it was from the heart and he commanded the respect of everybody in the team room, as anybody with his record should. He talked a lot to his lieutenants, Peter Baker, Des Smyth, D.J. Russell and Sandy Lyle, but generally just kept a close eye on everybody, watching to see how they coped with the build-up, looking for any tell-tale signs of anybody who might be getting nervous or worried about the challenge confronting them. I don't think he spotted much untoward. Everybody seemed fine – relaxed and looking forward to it. Woosie just let us get on with it. He knew we were as determined to win as he was.

What we wanted on Wednesday was for the atrocious weather to relent, but initially the course was closed and spectators were not allowed for safety reasons. Woosie sent us back to bed, or away to relax for a while, and then we got a message to say that we would be teeing off at 11.30.

We were all aware just how much many people had paid for the Ryder Cup experience and we didn't want to short change them, even though there was precious little to be gained from practising in such bad conditions. It would have been very harsh on the spectators who had paid just for that one day to be denied every-thing that they had been looking forward to, so we were all happy to go out and do what we could.

It wasn't really worth practising a lot, but we did our bit. After that, all we had to do for the rest of the day was prepare for that evening's gala dinner, one of the two events of the week that I was least looking forward, the opening ceremony being the other. Again, they both had to be faced and I would get through them.

When I came out of my room, dressed in black trousers, white dinner jacket, white shirt and red bow tie, all I needed to look like a proper magician was a top hat and three rabbits tucked up my sleeve. I had not gone many steps before I bumped into Dave Cannon, one of Getty Images' top photographers, who is a great bloke and always got on well with Heather. He asked me to pose with a group of the wives, so I sat down with all of them around me, and the image went round the world. It was another of those strange moments, but it was nice to have my picture taken with all of them. Very sadly, there was one wife missing.

I knew that the gala dinner was going to be another emotional moment, but I couldn't really prepare for it. There were 1,100 people in that dining room and every one of them knew my situation.

We came up with a master plan. Four of us were on our own – Monty, Chema, Dangerous and me – so we thought we would pair up, but when we were told that each of the single Americans had walked in on his own, I decided that was the way to go. I'd do it on my own.

They asked me where I wanted to go in the order and I said I might as well go last. I wasn't quite anticipating the reception, but I did get through it. For me, it was another tiny, yet significant, step of which there have been many, with many to come.

I must admit that it was very difficult with Heather not being at my side, but I did it. Lee's wife, Laurae, was there and as great as ever. Paul's wife, Ali, one of Heather's best friends, was fantastic then and throughout the week, as were all the wives or partners of both sides. Whenever Paul wasn't playing, Ali was watching me, and she was always there at the end of a round to make sure I was all right.

My mum and dad, Godfrey and Hetty, were at the gala dinner, together with my sister, Andrea, and her husband, Davy, and my aunt and uncle, Cynthia and Winston. That was helpful because I hadn't seen any of them all week and was able to catch up and be reassured that many who were closest to me were there and supportive. Two of my oldest friends, Dad's friends Raymond McGerr and Boyd Hunter, who used to help take me around when I played in Dungannon, where I had started my golfing career, were also there. It was good to be surrounded by so many of my family and friends.

The only thing that was disappointing about the dinner, which I think for me consisted of two pints of Guinness and very little blotting paper, was that, unlike previous ones, we were not roped off to allow us the chance to at least eat our food in peace. The Ryder Cup is a showpiece and it was very difficult to eat anything because of the tradition of getting all the players to sign menus. Every time you lifted a fork, somebody would be there saying, 'I'm sorry to interrupt you, but would you mind . . .' If they were sorry, they should have at least waited until we'd finished our food, but it was impossible and it became a bit overwhelming.

There was a steady stream of autograph- and photograph-hunters all night long, so much so that the Americans had to get bodyguards to stop people coming over, which looked a little offensive at the time, but wasn't meant to be. None of us has any issue with signing autographs, but there is a time and a place and the dinner table is not one of them.

The only other slight inconvenience was that we had to leave singer Van Morrison's set before it had finished. I have a very wide music base, but I've always been a huge fan of his because he's from home and sings some great songs. The only stuff of his I don't really enjoy is some of the blues, but that's the kind of music I usually walk out on wherever I am. I don't know why but jazz/blues just winds me up the wrong way and, apparently, it's the truest form of music. I just don't get it at all but, unfortunately, that's what he started with and, because every minute of our week is choreographed to the second and we have to stick to those timings, we had to leave before he'd finished, so we missed out on his standards. It wasn't quite right either that we left while he was still on stage, but unfortunately it happened.

We had travelled about half an hour by coach to the Citywest Hotel for the dinner and the Garda were there again afterwards to escort us back to the K Club – how wonderful it would be to have such an escort all the time, because it would take no time to get anywhere.

I boarded the bus and again the empty seat beside me was not what I was used to and felt particularly strange, but at least the difficult night was over. I felt I had done the right thing – stood up and been counted.

From start to finish of the whole week it was difficult for me to keep my emotions in check. I had to fight very hard, particularly at times when I was told what Tiger and Tom Lehman had said publicly about my participation. Tom said, 'I think having Darren here means a great deal, probably to him personally and to his team-mates, as well as to the US team and all the fans. I think having him as part of it makes this Ryder Cup significantly better. When it comes right down to it, we're all human beings, and whether or not we're playing in the Ryder Cup, you see a man who has had a tragedy like he's had to go through and you have an incredible amount of empathy for him.'

Support like that is just fantastic. That I managed to choke back my emotions, at least until after my singles match was over, wasn't because I wasn't cut up inside. I was still in the process of grieving but sometimes you just have to step out of it and get on with things, and that's what I was doing. It was still nice to get that night over – another little step in the healing process.

A colourful performer graces the opening ceremony.

5 | THURSDAY, 21 September

The whole thing about the Ryder Cup – early arrival and a Friday start, practice sessions and functions – is that it makes for a very long week, but as soon as the matches start, everything flies by . . . as long as the weather holds up.

It is difficult to forecast the weather in Ireland, even when the nearest cloud is in Nova Scotia, but we were warned that the tail end of a hurricane was on its way and that there was a possibility the matches might have to go into Monday. We didn't want that, and were not looking forward to it. We wanted to determine which was the better team as quickly as possible. A suggestion came from somewhere that we might have to play Friday's matches behind closed doors if the weather made it potentially dangerous for spectators. I didn't pay any attention to that, and I very much doubt that anybody would have allowed the matches to go ahead in front of empty stands. It is an exhibition, after all.

We were still pretty relaxed as we headed for the practice range for the final time before battle commenced, and Woosie came over to have a quick word with me. I asked him if I was playing on the first morning and he said that I would partner Lee in the fourballs. I said, 'Thank you very much. That will be all right. I won't let you down.' I didn't ask him about the afternoon – it was no use getting ahead of myself.

That was it. The Clarke-Westwood tandem would be in operation again and we were ready for anybody whom America would pitch against us. It was only after the opening ceremony and later in the evening that I enquired further into the captain's intentions, and told him my feelings.

I told Woosie that I knew he was going to have some tough decisions to make about what to do, because he had twelve fantastic players from whom to select. 'If you are watching things in the morning, not quite sure what's going on and debating what to do, then I am more than happy to sit out the afternoon session,' I told him. 'I will play whenever you want me to, but if you are in a predicament and want to get all the guys out on the first day, then I'll willingly stand down.'

I've been in situations in previous Ryder Cups when guys, including myself, haven't played and they haven't been happy and taken it the wrong way. I saw the bigger picture. We were all there as a team and I realised that Woosie might want everybody involved on the first day. I had no issues with playing in the morning, doing a bit of practice and then going out walking and supporting in the afternoon. I told him that he would have no problem with me if that was what he decided because I was quite happy to do it.

Whether that made any difference to his decisions I have no idea, but I didn't play either of the first two afternoons and it didn't worry me one bit. I was only doing what I would have wanted a player to say to me had I been captain. I may not have said that in previous Ryder Cups, because I wanted to play every session, but that was then and this was now.

After our final practice session, we retired to the locker room to prepare for the opening ceremony, the other function I was particularly wary about. I'd got through the gala dinner reasonably comfortably, so there was no reason why this should be any different, although there would be a much bigger audience.

We were in a holding area behind the stage. Wives and partners, all sporting their pink breast cancer awareness bows, had already taken their places. When it was our turn to enter the proceedings, we went up in alphabetical order, while the Americans chose world-ranking order. We were very comfortable with alphabetical order. In Ryder Cup week there is no favouritism shown towards anybody in the European side – not that I suspect there is with the Americans, either.

We don't have a pecking order, although I must say that every-body looks to Monty as our number-one player in the Ryder Cup, as he has been for so many times. He's a natural leader in this event and it won't be the same whenever he's not there. He's fantastic against America and just raises his game every single time. Everybody in our team room looked upon him as our leader and he deserved it. For him to be sitting in the middle on the stage, just like the letter M's position in the alphabet, says a lot about our team and the way that we think and perform.

With the weather we had endured for the previous two days, it was amazing that the sun came out for the opening ceremony, but it did. It all went very well and when all the speeches were done, everything was sorted and the first morning's fourballs announced, there was a change in the format for leaving.

President of Ireland, Mary McAleese, was centre stage and after she walked off we followed. Woosie and Tom went with their wives on the outside, Paul Casey went next with Tiger and partners, and I was next, accompanying the Mickelsons. Instead of me standing next to Phil, with Amy on the outside, we'd walked about five yards when Amy, who is such a lovely girl and another good friend of Heather's, came and stood between us and linked one of our arms each. She said, 'I do wish Heather was still here.' It was a huge gesture and that made the walk so much easier for me. Amy was absolutely wonderful then and all week, a really class act.

After the opening ceremony, we had a rules meeting, as we do at every Ryder Cup. The discussion was about whether we should be able to lift, clean and place our balls. The weather had left the fairways pretty wet and the balls would attract quite a bit of excess baggage when they landed.

I'm a stickler for the rules and believe in them absolutely 100 per cent because they are there for the purpose of keeping us all on the straight and narrow. However, when the course is wet, we get what are called mud balls, and when you hit a ball with mud on it, it comes off the clubface in very strange directions. A ball can take off, travel 30 yards right and then veer 40 yards to the left. If mud is on the left of the ball, it tends to fly right and, conversely, it flies left if the mud is on the right. Mud takes away the physics of the golf ball and you can't accurately predict what your ball is going to do. You only get mud balls on the fairway, hardly ever in the rough, so a player gets penalised for hitting good shots. That's why we play, clean and place at times, and that's why there was a debate about what we should do.

We are a showpiece, twenty-four of the best players in the world and we are there to play matchplay golf, not some kind of endurance game. This was my thinking. To me, if people come to watch the Ryder Cup, the British Masters or any event at an inland venue where it's a bit wet, they want to see us making birdies all over the place. They don't want to see us hitting what they think are terrible shots because we've pulled out a four or five iron and the ball's flown straight right. People often don't understand that we can't control the ball when there is a clump of mud on it. They see us as professionals who should be able to hit excellent shots at least 90 per cent of the time. We are supposed to hit it down the fairway and then close to the pin, and that's what people pay their money to see. With the Ryder Cup being an exhibition and not counting on any order of merit, I had no problem with lift, clean and place.

The other thing about being able to lift and clean is that it is exactly the same for your opponents as it is for you and offers no advantage to either side. A few of us put this case forward but at first the rules official could not commit to clean and place. Fortunately, somebody must have listened a little to our argument because they eventually relented and introduced lift, clean and place all week. Nobody in the team room disagreed, but maybe if I hadn't been playing my fifth Ryder Cup I would have sat there and kept quiet. As a senior player I felt I had a right to express my views.

We had a short team meeting afterwards when Woosie's basic message was, 'Go play.' It was no more complicated than that. That night was a private one in the team room and, with all the functions finished, we were out in jeans, T-shirts or whatever we wanted to wear. We knew who was playing whom the next day and Woosie went through everything with us, although everything wasn't all that much. It really was a case of 'just go play'. There were no specifics. 'The majority of you have been in this situation before and know what to do, so just go do it, because you're all playing great.' Everybody was relaxed and eager to get going.

Monty was laughing and joking to ease what little tension there might have been, but really everybody was at peace with themselves and the situation. We were totally united. Woosie's relaxed attitude towards the week worked well throughout it, although I suspect he was not quite as relaxed as he appeared in front of us. He was having to make decisions all the time, and be here, there and everywhere and do bits and pieces with the team, but he came across as very calm. If he had any doubts or concerns, they were not transmitted to us. All the vice-captains and assistants kept a close eye on us in practice, but their job was made that much easier by the fact that we were all playing well. It does make a difference.

For example, Paul McGinley, who had been struggling coming into the week, suddenly got a massive injection of confidence and played brilliantly all week. Although I was short on match practice, I had the confidence of having put in many a long day on the range at home with my coach, Ewen Murray. I knew my game was in shape. I was confident that I could do what I had come here to do, and I had the support of everybody – those in the American camp as well – which only went to show how much everybody thought and cared about Heather.

It was lights out at 10.10 for me, but I forgot one very important thing.

Jose Maria Olazabal and Sergio Garcia get Europe off the mark.

6 | FRIDAY, 22 September

I rarely have a problem sleeping, although I do wake up early, which is just as well. I have had one or two sleepless nights at the Ryder Cup, but the previous night had not been one of them. For somebody with as structured a day-to-day carry-on as I have, I had committed the unpardonable error of forgetting to set my alarm clock. I was supposed to be downstairs at 6.45 for an 8.45 start, but woke at 6.20. I'm a strict time-keeper and thought, 'Oh hell,' or words to that effect, 'I'll have to rush around doing everything.' Our clothes are all so organised for us, though, that my most difficult task was deciding which colour boxer shorts I should wear – black or white.

We have a book telling us what colour outfits we have to wear each day, but somebody usually forgets to look and gets his red confused with blue. When they come into the team room they always stand out and get plenty of stick, but everybody seemed to be colour co-ordinated on the first day. The outfit was, very fittingly, emerald green.

The atmosphere was a little more apprehensive than it had been, but people were looking forward to getting going at last. There was total commitment to the cause. Rarely can a European team have had its confidence at a better level. What was more, although we had respect for them, there was no fear of those we would be facing across the tee.

I had thought about everything long and hard after Heather passed away, and since Woosie gave me the nod everything had been a build-up to this first morning. My mantra was simply – Friday morning at the K Club, Friday morning at the K Club.

Walking out on to the range on that Friday morning was for me a matter of chest out, stomach in, walk tall, you have a job to do. My trusty friend and aide Lee was close at hand. Lee's usually three steps behind me because he struggles to keep up, being a little bit heavy these days, but he's always there. He's an unbelievable partner and one of whom you could not ask anything more. We have this ease with one another that if I mess up a hole, I have 110 per cent conviction that he's fine on his own, and vice versa. He has no problem with leaving me on my own. It's obviously much better if you are both in the hole, but it sometimes doesn't happen like that in Ryder Cup. We know each other and our game so well that we have no issue and no reason to say, 'Sorry, partner.' To have him walking alongside me was all that I needed and made it so much easier for me.

There had been a little bit of criticism about Woosie picking both of us, so we had a point to prove. We have played well together before and the two of us are not afraid of anybody – absolutely anybody.

On the range, I was fine warming up and then hitting a few putts and chips. I was judging everything perfectly, which was good because you don't want to spend too much time on the 1st tee. I knew I was ready, so I turned to Lee and said, 'Okay partner, let's go.' He was hitting another couple of putts, so I repeated, 'Come on, Lee. I'm ready, let's go. Come on,' but still he waited, said nothing, then picked his balls out of the hole and off we went.

The crowds in the stands all roared as we walked off and then, halfway across from the putting green, for some unknown reason, Lee ran ahead of me. I wondered where he was going. Did he need the toilet? Why was he abandoning me in my hour of need? I thought, 'Don't do that, partner. I need you here beside me,' but he had disappeared round the corner and walked on to the bottom bit of the tee.

It was only when I rounded the corner and came into the full glare of the crowd and spotlight that I realised what he had been doing. Lee was standing there leading the clapping.

Walking through the gap with all those people shouting and roaring, the noise was just deafening. I couldn't even begin to explain my feelings at the time. Obviously, a lot of them were emotional because Heather wasn't there to see it, a lot of them were because I was so proud to be part of this team in Ireland and on top of that was gratitude for the support of the crowd because I had chosen to be there. The roar was unbelievable. I have been to many tournaments around the world and I have not heard a louder one. It was a cacophony of sound. I just looked up at everybody and nobody and said, 'Thank you.'

I could see my caddie Billy Foster's eyes were welling up. He has been with me for ten years, through thick and thin, with a little break, and two years ago he lost his mother to cancer. Billy has always been a shoulder to cry on, always been there for me, will always be there for me and he knew what it meant. As well as being a great person, he's one of the best caddies in the world. Tiger would not have asked him to caddy for him during the President's Cup had he not been. Both he and Lee were damp-eyed on the tee and if I'd known at the time I would have dipped into my bag and handed them a Kleenex each. I may not have been totally fine, but I was definitely fine.

Inside I was saying to myself, 'Keep yourself together. This is the Ryder Cup. You have to perform. You are going to perform. Please, let me hit the ball.' My heart was racing and all sorts of emotions were going through every part of my body.

Our opponents, Phil Mickelson and Chris DiMarco, came on to the tee thirty seconds later and they both gave me hugs and said, 'Darren, it's fantastic you're here.' It was above and beyond what they had to say and do. Normally, you just shake hands and say, 'Play well.' I'm not a guy-hugging sort of chap, that's just not me, but in those circumstances it seemed right. If I can have two guys like Phil and Chris giving me a hug on the 1st tee, that's what the Ryder Cup is all about. It's not about animosity. It's about a match between friends that we both want to win. Chris and Phil merely did what the entire European and American teams did all week and that was to show me their great sympathy and affection. It was so very kind of them.

Somebody subsequently wrote in the media that there were tears from me on the 1st tee. I did not shed one tear, not one, because I could not afford to let myself go but the press had decided it would make a better story if they wrote that I did – so they did, but I didn't.

Chris and Phil hit off first, as the visitors. Lee asked if I wanted him to go and I said, 'No thanks, I'm ready, I'll go.'

I looked at Billy and said, 'The wind's against and from the left, so shall I hit a little three wood or what? Is it a three wood or what is it?' But before he could answer, I said, 'No, give me the driver. I'm not going to come all the way here and hit a three wood. I've got a shot to hit so give me the driver.'

As I prepared, I just thought to myself, 'There are so many people wondering where this is going to go . . . and I'm one of them. Am I going to top hit, hit it straight, right or left, or even miss it altogether?' I just stood there and said to myself, 'This is it. This is your job. This is what you do. This is what you have done all these years. Now do it.'

It was obviously nerve-wracking and there were a lot of things going through my head, so I just repeated, 'Give me the driver. What's the run out?' Billy said it was 340.

I had been watching the screens on the range and seen where everybody was hitting it, where people were finishing if they took a three wood or a driver. Now I had made my choice and it was my turn. We had gone from deafening roars to cathedral calm. One minute you needed earplugs and the next you could hear a feather land on a pillow. I just stood tall, went through my pre-shot routine, took the club back and then just absolutely nutted the ball. I killed it down the middle, some 340 yards, to just before the run-out at the end of the fairway.

The beauty of that tee shot was not how and where I hit it, but what I learned from it. Now I know that if I ever get in a position again where the pressure is that much and I have to front it, I can

The victory at Valderrama in 1997 was my first taste of the Ryder Cup. *Left to right, back row*: Colin Montgomerie, Jesper Parnevik, Lee Westwood, Ignacio Garrido, Nick Faldo. *Middle row*: Darren Clarke, Per-Ulrik Johansson, Seve Ballesteros, Bernhard Langer, Thomas Bjorn. *Front row*: Costantino Rocca, Jose Maria Olazabal, Ian Woosnam.

Mark James was a fantastic captain at Brookline in 1999 but we were outplayed on the final day. *Left to right, back row*: Sergio Garcia, Miguel Angel Jimenez, Padraig Harrington, Darren Clarke, Jarmo Sandelin, Andrew Coltart, Jesper Parnevik, Jean Van de Velde. *Front row*: Sam Torrance, Lee Westwood, Jose Maria Olazabal, Mark James, Colin Montgomerie, Paul Lawrie, Ken Brown.

Sam Torrance was the hero at The Belfry in 1985 and we wanted to win for him so much when he was captain in 2002. *Left to right, back row*: Mark James, Joakim Haeggman, Padraig Harrington, Thomas Bjorn, Colin Montgomerie, Jesper Parnevik, Darren Clarke, Niclas Fasth, Phillip Price. *Front row*: Sergio Garcia, Lee Westwood, Paul McGinley, Sam Torrance, Ian Woosnam, Pierre Fulke, Bernhard Langer.

Bernhard Langer's thoroughness helped us to a record win at Oakland Hills in 2004. *Left to right, back row*: Miguel Angel Jimenez, Padraig Harrington, Darren Clarke, Bernhard Langer, Colin Montgomerie, Thomas Levet, Ian Poulter. *Front row*: Lee Westwood, Paul McGinley, Luke Donald, Sergio Garcia, Paul Casey, David Howell.

I decided to stop playing after the Open Championship at Hoylake. It was not a difficult decision.

Heather, who was so courageous and uncomplaining.

Ian Woosnam gave me the signal to get my spikes back on by selecting me as one of his wild cards.

Facing the media for the first time since Heather's death was one of the hardest things I have ever had to do.

Carding a 68 in the first round of the Madrid Open, my first tournament for two months, showed my game was in decent shape.

Captain Woosie was in charge of the Ryder Cup but, fortunately, not the plane.

We all assemble at Dublin Airport, although we arrived on different aeroplanes. *Clockwise, from top right*: Henrik Stenson, Jose Maria Olazabal, Padraig Harrington, Paul Casey, Lee Westwood, Colin Montgomerie, Ian Woosnam, Glendryth Woosnam, Darren Clarke, Paul McGinley, David Howell, Luke Donald, Sergio Garcia, Robert Karlsson.

Welcome to Dublin – Tom Lehman leads his team off the plane. *Clockwise, from top right*:
JJ Henry, Zach Johnson, Scott Verplank, Chris DiMarco, Loren Roberts, Vaughn Taylor,
Tom Lehman, Melissa Lehman, Corey Pavin, Chad Campbell, David Toms, Brett Wetterich,
Stewart Cink.

Facing the media again, this time at the K Club, I am able to raise the odd smile.

Opposing captains Ian Woosnam and Tom Lehman undergo the first of many grillings from the media during the week.

The lovely K Club Hotel overlooks the River Liffey. Some of the players even found time to go fishing before the action began.

Rain in Ireland? Surely not. Zach Johnson is prepared.

Phil Mickelson is the first of the Americans on the practice range.

Greeting Tiger for the first time since the Open was a special moment.

Practising on Tuesday at the 16th – Westwood and I took the money off Harrington and McGinley.

waiting was over, I was back to the day job. I had no idea what to expect, I just didn't know how things would work out especially on that first hole, but Heather was definitely watching out for me.

I didn't have a sense of destiny. It was just a question of doing what I had to do. I had no idea I was going to shoot 3 on the first hole – it could easily have been 6. I was just determined to get on with things as much as I could and play as well as I could. Lee was fantastic and we ham and egged like we normally do. He holed some great putts and I holed some to keep us going.

We knew it was going to be a tight game against one of their best teams, but even at the height of the contest the occasional amusing moment arises when you can forget the importance of what you are doing and have a chuckle. Ours came on the 4th green when Billy forgot that, although my ball was off the green, we could lift, clean and place it. He was just having a little time to himself, enjoying the scenery, looking at everybody in the stands and having a nice time without worrying about me having my ball cleaned. Thankfully, John Graham, Lee's caddie, was there with his towel so we all had a little joke at Billy's expense.

It was no laughing matter trying to beat Phil and Chris, though, and we could never shake them off. Both teams kept the other going.

On the par-5 16th, I hit a great five wood just off the back fringe and Lee had also hit two great shots on to the green. I chipped mine stone dead so we were still one up, a position we maintained after finishing the very tough 17th, where my partner and I both had putts to win the game, but missed.

It was impossible for us to lose, but there was no relief in knowing that, because the difference between a half and a full point can be massive in the overall picture. There were a couple of instances in other matches when it looked as though America was going to get something back on the 18th, but Paul Casey and Monty both holed great putts to make sure the momentum stayed with us. It was the same with Lee and me. We wanted to make sure we didn't give anything away. You don't want to lose the last hole. You just want to do what you have to do. I hit a very good tee shot and the flag was in the right back corner, a position we had played to many times before. I took a little bit off a five wood, and held it against the wind. It was a good shot, which came down just off the edge of the green, just 15 feet away. I knew it was a two-putt 4.

Phil hit in the most glorious shot, straight at the flag, but it had just a little bit too much club and, because of where the pin was, he would have to come back over a hump, making for an unbelievable shot if he holed it for a 3. He didn't, so then I had this 15-footer, which I had to get down in 2.

The putt looked good most of the way and I thought I had holed it at one stage, but it rolled a little bit past. As usual, I had been slightly nervous over it. It was just four inches past the hole and the Americans said, 'Pick it up.'

The game was over. The two captain's picks had their first point on the board, the perfect start. We had been up against one of America's strongest pairings but had been good enough to win and, thankfully, I had contributed. There were hugs all round, and I also got one from Phil's wife Amy, but the one person I really wanted a hug from wasn't there. I really missed Heather at that moment.

I don't know whether they have ever put two wild cards out

together before, but Woosie had faith in us and we'd started to repay him. There was such a sense of relief that I'd gone out there, done it, and performed. I had known for six weeks that that was exactly what I had to do. I'd promised myself, and those who had listened to me in Madrid, that I would get myself through the week. So far I thought I'd done that pretty well.

I had to present myself to the media again and I answered all the questions about everything that had happened, and then somebody asked, 'When you holed that putt on the 18th green, what were your emotions?' I had bared my soul for the previous two weeks and for some reason I thought this was a step too far, a question too many. I looked at my questioner and thought I'm not going to give him the answer that I'd like to and say what I'd like to say because that's what he's probably looking for anyway. So I just said, 'Ones that I hope you will never have to face.' I didn't mean it as a put down, but I felt better after I'd said it to him. He had just overstepped the mark, but I'm sure he had not realised it.

I walked out of the media centre, took my boots off and went out on the course to support the others. I didn't watch anybody in particular but just walked around to see what was happening and lend support where it might be needed. It was not easy because I was very wary about walking towards greens where hundreds of people were sitting in stands. All the spectators were roaring me on, even though I was not playing. I didn't want them to put people off when they were playing shots.

I had to put my hands up a couple of times to control the crowds. The week wasn't about me and I didn't want it to be. Some of it was to do with me and there was a lot going on around me, but this was the Ryder Cup. Europe were playing America. I wasn't comfortable at all that a lot of people seemed to be turning it round towards me. I didn't want it or seek it. We were there as a team, so I was careful about not using the crowd to my advantage by fist pumping or anything like that. I tried to be very respectful to our opponents. When people clapped, I put my hand up and acknowledged them, but I wasn't firing them up. I wouldn't have done anything detrimental to my opponents. I loved it that people were showing me their support, I thought the world of them for doing it, but I didn't want the whole tournament turned around to be about me.

Watching all the games, I could tell that the guys were playing simply fantastic golf. There was a slight distraction on one hole when I saw one of my all-time heroes, Michael Jordan, a big golf fan and one of Tiger's best friends. I've got pictures of MJ in my gym from when he was playing for the Chicago Bulls and I know he likes a cigar, just like I do. I was walking behind the 16th when he called out to me and asked if I had any cigars. When I said no, he dipped into his pocket and handed me one of my favourites, a Hoyo de Monterey double corona. So we chatted away and he was asking how the boys were doing and how I was doing. MJ's a top bloke and he said that when he was next over in London he'd like to go for a game and meet the two boys. You wouldn't want to fall out with him because he's got the biggest hands I've ever seen. When you shake hands with him, yours simply disappears, all the way up to your elbow.

Back to the golf, it was different for me, walking around following the team, because, apart from my first Ryder Cup when I thought I was going to go three days without a game, I think I've played in every session since then. At least, if Woosie decided to play me both sessions on Saturday, I'd have had a little bit of rest and would be a bit fresher than I would have been in the past before going into the Sunday singles. It was great for me to be able to go out there and see my team-mates perform, particularly as they were doing it so magnificently.

Woosie had to make some big calls when you think that he'd left out Luke Donald from the morning fourballs and he's number nine in the world. David Howell also sat out and he was number two in Europe at the time.

I enjoyed every minute of it and I felt I'd done my bit for the team. At the end of the day everybody had contributed to the points score, which was a superb achievement after just one day. All twelve players had won at least half a point. That was just huge.

Woosie told me I'd been picked to play with Lee again the following morning. We were to go out third and were facing Tiger and Jim Furyk. Lee said, 'That's fine, we'll be all right' – not in an arrogant way, but just because both of us love playing against the best players in the world. One of our greatest memories together is when we played and beat Tiger and David Duval in the 1999 Ryder Cup when they were number one and two in the world. We managed to sneak a win there. We simply love the challenge.

Everybody was a bit tired during dinner that night because there had been a lot of emotion involved and adrenalin flowing. When I went to bed my head was swimming with all kinds of thoughts but the prominent one was how much I wished Heather was there to share it with me.

It was another one of those moments when I got into bed and realised she wasn't there. It's hard to describe the ache when you get into a bed you've been used to sharing for such a long time and there's nobody there. Heather loved the Ryder Cup. She wasn't there and I had to get on with it. I had no choice.

I came back to reality quickly when I realised that, while everything had been going on during the day, I hadn't had a chance to speak to the boys because they were back at school, so I rectified that. Tyrone had been told at school by one of his teachers that I'd won my match, while Conor wasn't particularly bothered. He just said, 'Well done, Daddy,' and then started chatting about Lego and his Playstation game.

Zach Johnson celebrates winning his morning fourball by chipping in at the 17th hole.

7 | SATURDAY, 23 September

It was much easier walking on to the 1st tee second time around than it had been on that first morning. The crowd still went wild, but it wasn't as it had been on the first morning, and I was happy because I was back in my workplace, just doing my job.

When I see Tiger across the tee, it's not intimidating, just thrilling. If you can't get up for playing the game against the best, you might as well retire. On this day, as it turned out, he had a really, really off one, and we weren't complaining. It was totally out of character for him because he didn't play anywhere near to the standard that we all know he can. However, he was still playing with Jim Furyk, who had not got to number two in the world for no reason, and Jim was very steady and strong as ever.

When you're playing against Tiger and Jim, you have to grasp the momentum when the opportunity arises. On this occasion we didn't. Lee had missed a couple of chances on the 2nd and 3rd holes – not that he hadn't made a good stroke each time, they just weren't destined to drop. So when we got to the 4th and he was 25 feet away from the hole and I'd wedged to four feet, I decided to go first when it was our team's shot because we didn't want him missing another. They hadn't been going in for him and I didn't want him to see another one stay out. I'm not sure if it would have affected him, but it was one of those things we didn't want to test.

Anyway, I holed the putt to give us the lead and then got a couple of halves on the next two holes, so walking on to the 7th hole I said to Lee, 'You've done the first three, I've done the second three, so now it's your turn again.' Actually, we were both coming in and out okay.

We thought Tiger was going to get one back on the 9th, but he must have misread the putt and just lipped out. On the 11th I hit a tee shot right over a bunker and then hit an eight iron to about four feet and that put us three up. Lee and Tiger both hit great shots into the next but both missed their putts. Then Lee hit a fine shot into the par 3 to get a birdie and put us four up. Although Lee hit another great shot into the next, Jim holed his putt and Lee missed his to take us to the 16th at dormie three.

Sixteen is a reachable hole for Tiger but it's on the limit for us, and Jim probably can't reach it. As it happened, we all laid up. Lee hit a decent shot in, but the wind caught it and after a couple of bounces it went into the water off the side of the green. It was down to me and I'd laid up just a little in the first cut. Jim hit a great shot in there with fantastic spin control to about eight feet and I hit a good wedge, but it ended up just over the back of the green. Tiger put his a similar distance to Jim's ball, so I'm walking round the back of the green thinking we might lose this hole and 17's a bit of a smelly one where anything could happen. We didn't want to have been four up with four to go and have to play 18.

When I got to my ball, the lie was just perfect. We didn't want to give them the hole without a fight, so it was imperative that I got up and down at least. I'd been working very hard with Ewen Murray on my short game, straightforward little chips and from all ranges, and as soon as I hit the ball, I knew it couldn't go anywhere else but the hole.

I don't go along with the destiny thing, but it was one of those moments when I knew it was going to be my week. It was a case of wow, we've done it again. We were fortunate that Tiger had had an off day, but we'd still won our first two matches. You never want to beat the best player in the world on one of his off days, but when it comes to the Ryder Cup, you take whatever you can.

We were interviewed afterwards by Sky's Dominic Holyer and asked about how the two picks felt. I said there were a lot of people out there worrying about Woosie's two wild cards but, you know, we're all right. The only ones who weren't worried were Lee and me. I think we'd just proved that. After we'd finished, I asked Woosie if I was playing again in the afternoon and he said to take another rest, which I was fine about.

Just as on the first day, everybody was playing as if they were unbeatable in the afternoon and at one stage it looked like we were going to win all four foursomes, but it didn't quite work out that way. We'd still won the series, which made it four out of four – all four series had been won 2½–1½ – and we needed only another 4½ points to win the Cup for the fifth time in six matches. We had to be very careful not to get ahead of ourselves as we did at Brookline in 1999 when we had gone into the last day leading by exactly the same margin. There was a difference here, and a big one. Unlike at Brookline, everybody here was on top of his game right from the start.

We knew this time that America could top load their order, bottom load it, or do whatever they wanted to do, because it wasn't going to affect our team. We had a good lead, everybody was playing well and there was not one player on our team who felt that they could not beat anybody in their team. That's just the way we felt. It didn't make any difference which way the draw came out. Woosie did not ask me where I wanted to play – he knew I would play wherever he wanted me to – but he did ask me who I thought should go off first. I said it would make no difference, but the natural number one was Monty, a position he had made his own.

When the draw came up we were in the team room and I was at number seven against Zach Johnson. It took me a while to realise it, but I suddenly thought, 'It might be me. It might come down to me making the putt that wins the Ryder Cup.' I wasn't the only one with those thoughts because Paul McGinley said to me, 'You know, it could be either me or you.' I didn't know if Woosie had put me there for that reason, because that would have been getting ahead of ourselves, but it was quite exciting to think that the whole Ryder Cup could finish with the outcome of my match.

We had a brief team meeting that night and Woosie just said to us, 'Whatever you do, don't think ahead, just do what you have to do. Just concentrate on your own game.'

When I went to bed that night, I thought to myself, I've contributed to the team. I've done okay. My life had become a series of little steps, and that was another one.

Celebrating with Henrik Stenson, the man who holed the putt that won the Ryder Cup for Europe.

8 | SUNDAY, 24 September

We got a little bit of a lie in because the singles matches don't start until later, and what a difference those extra two hours made. We were all bright-eyed by breakfast time. There was a real air of optimism, but not over-confidence, because we were all too aware of history.

Woosie's instructions to us were, more simply, words of encouragement. He didn't have to say much, we were all playing well and the less he said the more it confirmed the trust he had in us. I was very aware that in four previous attempts I had not won a Ryder Cup singles. Phil beat me at Valderrama, Hal Sutton beat me at Brookline, David Duval holed a 15-footer on the last green at the Belfry to get a half with me, and the last one was against Davis Love, who is one of my best friends, at Oakland Hills.

At Oakland Hills, it was almost as if Davis and I contrived a half. I missed from three feet for the win, after being two down with three to play.

I birdied 16 to get back to one down and chipped in on the 17th to square the match, while Davis did something on the last hole that was just typical of him. He pulled his tee shot into the thick rough, not that that was typical, close to a drainage grate. He could have stood on it and got relief, but he wouldn't because he thinks the same way as I do about the rules. From the lie he had, his only shot was to pitch it back into play, while I was in much better shape and hit a five iron on to the green. Davis played a pretty decent pitch to about 15 feet, while my first putt was a good one, though it headed about a yard past the hole.

I was standing on the edge of the green, thinking that I'd love to give Davis the putt. Why don't I just go over there and say, 'Good, good,' and we'd settle for a half?

Unfortunately, there were no scoreboards in view on the 18th, so I didn't know what the overall picture was. I didn't want to put the team in a position of losing a half point if we were struggling. To this day, I wish I'd gone and given it to him, and I told both caddies at the side of the green I wanted to, but by the time I'd decided that was the best thing to do, he was already standing over his putt addressing the ball. I didn't want to beat Davis. He didn't want to beat me. You want to win, yes, but I was playing against one of my best friends, who is an unbelievably good guy.

As it turned out, he missed his putt so I had the three-footer to beat him. It was quite a weird sensation as I stood over it. I didn't really want to hole the putt and there are not many times in a golfer's career that this happens. In the event, it just lipped out on the bottom side and, in my mind, justice was done. I was delighted that we had a half because he deserved it. If I'd holed the putt, I'd have felt so guilty it would not have sat right with me at all. I don't think I'll ever be as unperturbed about not winning again in my entire career.

Back at the K Club, no matter who had played me that day would have found it very tough. The reception I got on that 1st tee will remain with me forever. The support was incredible. It must have been very hard for Zach, a really nice guy and a good player, with all the noise and support going for me.

We halved the first three and I made a good birdie on the 4th. He made a good 20-footer on the 5th to get back to all square and I made a good par on the next to go one up. Then Zach got a gust of wind that took his ball into the water on 7. So I went two up, halved the next in pars and then, on 9, I just told myself to concentrate and not get ahead of myself. I'd seen the scoreboard on the 9th and was still thinking that the fate of the Ryder Cup could come down to me. I holed a 35-footer over a hump to go three up on 10 and I looked at Billy and said, 'I don't believe this. This is a bit strange.'

At this stage, I was still in professional mode. We weigh up shots and decide whether to take them on or not, while we know the best idea is just to play percentage shots. This thinking does not sit easily with me, but sometimes it has to be done. Billy probably wishes I did it an awful lot more than I do.

I hit it on the right edge of the green on 12, some 150 feet from the hole, while Zach was only 20 feet away. Just make sure you get up and down and make him have to win it, was my only thinking, but when the ball went over the hump in the green, I thought actually this isn't bad. It was tracking for the hole. Then it broke left and I thought that's it, it's not going in, but then it broke back right and went straight into the middle of the hole. I could not believe I had just holed it. Zach was bound to miss after that, so now I was four up. That's when I really started thinking this could come down to me.

As soon as I was totally convinced that I was the one, if I won, who could roll in the putt to claim Sam Ryder's pot of gold again, my mind started to race. I'd kept my emotions in check all week, but now there was turmoil. I started to think about Heather watching and all kinds of things were in my head.

I came off my tee shot on 13 and hit into the rough, while Zach hit two good shots on to the green. I laid up short and pitched to four feet. I had the putt to stay four up, but my mind was not doing what it should be doing. I had got ahead of myself, which is one of the worst possible things you can do in golf. I missed and walked on to the 14th three up.

Zach was up first and pushed his shot a bit right. I stood up with a three iron and hit it straight down the flag, absolutely flushed it. It finished eight feet away, while Zach just missed his chip.

I'd got this one to be four up with four to go. I missed but it was a gimme, or at least it was to me. We had played the game in a fantastic spirit, but with my mind not functioning properly, I walked round and looked at Zach, expecting him to say it was good, but Zach was not going to give it to me. I look at him again and he said, 'Oh, all right, pick it up.' I wasn't meaning to be rude by looking at him. My mind just wasn't where it should have been.

So I was three up with four to go. I hit my tee shot on 15 into the rough and Zach followed me. I had a decent lie and got it on to 40 feet, just outside Zach. This putt was to win the game. I told myself to forget about the scoreboard and concentrate. I hit a fantastic putt and I've no idea how it stayed out, but it just shaved the left edge and was two inches away – three up, three to play.

Playing 16, my mind really was racing so far ahead I was in danger of lapping myself. Am I going to keep my emotions in check? Oh I do wish Heather was here with me. Come on, Darren, you've still got it to do.

I hit a good drive down 16, but neither of us could reach, so both had to lay up. I hit it on to the green – a 25-foot downhill, fast and left to right. Zach hit a good shot, but it spun back and he had an uphill chip from closer than mine.

As we walked round past the big stand, everybody in it was standing up, roaring and shouting. My other team mates were there, plus it looked like the entire population of Ireland. One more check on the scoreboard. I was still thinking this could be me, although I wasn't really sure what was going on. I was trying to keep my head in check, but I was struggling.

I hit my putt and, although it was a very fast one, I left it about two feet short. Zach was walking past and he said, 'I can't give you that, Darren.' That was fine by me. He burnt the left edge and now I had a two-footer to win the match and I was all over the place.

I started to wonder how I was going to get it into the hole. My mind had gone. Everything was coming into my head. I had a two-footer to win my game, possibly the Ryder Cup in Ireland, my first ever singles, and my wife's not here. I honestly didn't think I could hit the putt.

It was then that one of the most magnanimous gestures in Ryder Cup history occurred. I'm not sure if Zach realised my predicament, but he was not going to put me through any more turmoil. He walked round, picked up my marker and the match was over. It was an unbelievable gesture to do that in his first Ryder Cup.

My putt was easy to miss and I think he realised what a let down it would be in front of all those people if I did. I don't know if I would have holed it or not. I'd like to think that somehow I would have got it into the hole, but it was far from a done deal. Zach's gesture was magnificent and I will never forget that.

Zach gave me a hug, and when I turned to Billy, I just couldn't hold it back any more. Everything came flooding out. I was a mess. I had done what I had to do. I had got through the week and performed reasonably well. The whole week had been a success, in Ireland, and Heather wasn't there. I couldn't hang on any more. The floodgates opened and to hell with trying to close them.

Billy was there for me, as usual. He's so supportive of everything that I've done and that I do. At the end of the day, it's a fact of professional golf that we spend more time with our caddies than we do with our wives. I wouldn't be in the position I'm in today, or have achieved as much, without him, plus a few other people. He's the guy who walks the fairways with me and I can't imagine anybody else doing it. He knew exactly what I was going through. I had spoken to him when I was deciding whether or not to put myself up to play in the Ryder Cup. He was there the whole time.

We had a long hug and then Tom Lehman came over and gave me a hug and said some very special words to me. Woosie was crying as well and saying, 'It's destiny. It's destiny.' I just looked at him and said, 'Woosie, I told you I wouldn't let you down.'

I walked over to the side and the next person I bumped into was Tiger and he too said some wonderful words. He was understanding because of what we had both been through in recent times with our families. It was very, very emotional.

My mum, dad and Andrea were next, coming over and hugging me, and then I went towards the crowd to thank them. Afterwards, I received an unbelievable number of emails. Most people said that they were crying as much as I was. As I said earlier, I'm not into crying or guy hugs or anything like that, but on this occasion it seemed the most natural thing in the world to do.

It was very hard for me to have cameras in my face straight after the match was over. All the media attention was very hard. I did one interview, but then walked away to the side of the green to call the two boys at home. Tyrone had been watching most of it and Conor just a little bit. They were fine, but I was very disappointed to have some of my conversation with them repeated next day in the media. Two of the papers reported what I had said, although they had no idea what the kids had said. They must have heard me and decided to print it. That was an intrusion. They shouldn't have done it because it was a personal conversation.

I quickly realised soon after I'd won the match that it wasn't me who had claimed the Ryder Cup. Henrik Stenson had just beaten me to it. I wasn't the least bit worried about that. It would have been too much of a fairy tale for me to have holed it. As long as we won, I wasn't bothered, because we were there as a team. It was fantastic for Henrik, and I don't have any issue with that. The team had won and that was all that mattered.

In fact, there are those who claim that it was actually Luke Donald who did it because, with me and another match being dormie, we already had the 14½ points since Henrik and I were assured of a half point. It didn't matter who did it – *we* did it and it was just as good as it gets. For the Irish, it was pure genius.

Being part of this particular team had done a lot for me. It showed me how much people cared about me and that they cared for Heather, too, and that meant everything.

Doing all the television interviews and trying to keep myself in check and answer the questions, without Heather right beside me, was very difficult but I'd achieved it. As for Woosie, looking at the scoreboard and the amount of blue on it said everything about him as a captain.

I'll never forget the atmosphere of the crowd and everybody giving me a hug. I walked up 17 with Jose Maria, who was playing against Phil Mickelson, and when he won his game the first thing he did was burst into tears and give me a hug. He said he was so happy for me. I said likewise. He's one of the most genuine guys you will ever meet. He wears his heart on his sleeve and I can't speak highly enough about him. He's such a good fellow. I've practised with him in America and he's helped me so much, just a genuine top guy. I could ask him anything and he'd help me. While Heather was ill he'd always be sending messages, and when she passed away he was one of the first to get in touch. Heather got on fantastically with him.

He was also very emotional because he hadn't thought it would happen again for him. He hadn't played Ryder Cup for such a long time because of injury and other things, and now here he was, part of another winning team. He was in buckets of tears and being there with him was again one of those very special moments.

Then we walked down 18 with Lee, who was striving to hold off a comeback from Chris DiMarco. Lee had played so well again all week, but somehow he'd slipped under the radar and missed out on the general appreciation his play deserved. Once again he had been our joint top points scorer and unbeaten in his last two Ryder Cups with 8^1/2 points out of 10. People don't recognise just how well he does. Our selection as the two picks had been classed as a gamble in some quarters, but the two people who looked on it that way the least were Lee and me.

Chris made great birdies on 16 and 17, but hit a couple of bad shots on 18 and that was it. Lee had won 4 points out of 5 and got very little praise for it. That disappointed me. A lot of the attention had focused on me, which I hadn't wanted, so Lee didn't get the recognition he deserved for being a pick. That was very unfair.

It was a monumental team effort by everybody. We celebrated on the 18th green and champagne started flowing. I soaked Lee, he soaked me and everybody else wanted to christen me. It was spraying bubbles all over the place.

It was the first time since Heather passed away that I actually felt happy for a little bit, just a while. That was probably normal. I hadn't forgotten that she wasn't there. If she had been, I think she would have been proud of me.

Upstairs on the balcony, when we were posing for photographs, the Irish flag was wrapped around the three Irishmen in the team. Padraig was mindful of giving me the orange end. He knows the script.

Then Billy came out with a pint of Guinness for me, as it's known that I'm partial to a little drop of it now and again. He handed me the glass and as soon as I raised it up the crowd went mad and I had no option but to chuck it down in one – not that I wouldn't have done anyway. Woosie tried something similar, but more slowly.

We faced the press as a unit for the first and last time and Woosie proclaimed the week as the pinnacle of his sporting life. 'I've won many tournaments around the world, including a Major, and been number one, but I've got to say that this is the proudest moment of my life,' he said. 'When you have twelve fantastic players like these and the back-up staff I've had, then my job's been easy.' He admitted that he had arrived at the K Club without a specific game plan beyond just seeing how we were playing at the time. It was all the easier once he realised that everybody was on form.

'When they asked me to be captain eighteen months ago, any victory would have been fantastic, but to get the same record as Bernhard Langer did, is unbelievable – a dream come true. But I have been worried about it because it's an unbelievable responsibility to be captain. It's all right standing there as a player because the only person you can let down is yourself.

'But I had fantastic players and we could have had two teams out there. I'm not saying we would have got this result, but it shows the potential of European golf. We have strength and depth for a long time to come, and the future for the Ryder Cup is looking great for Europe.'

Paul McGinley, as ever, found appropriate words for the occasion. 'Heather would have been right in the middle of it if she'd been here. And Big D, you've been great this week and we're so proud of the way you've handled everything. Not only that, but the way you played as well. All credit, we're one big family and we miss Heather dearly.'

It was perhaps as well that we still had the closing ceremony, otherwise some might have been wrecked far earlier than they eventually were. We had all had a drink or two, but it was only when I was putting on my pink jacket that all of a sudden I realised its relevance. Nobody had said anything to me and I never twigged, even when I was bringing the clothes down – of course, it was the breast cancer awareness colour.

I doubt there was a dry eye in the house when Woosie dedicated the Ryder Cup to Heather and, after the closing ceremony was over, Phil and I walked off arm in arm with Amy.

Then it was into the top bar in the clubhouse where all our families had gathered. We were in there for an hour because there was no laid out agenda for that evening. It was just fun time. I wanted to go to the tented village to have a drink with the public, because the crowd had been so good to me during the week, but David Howell and Sergio had already been there and the crowd went so completely ballistic they were both manhandled. There had been all kinds of problems with security. I had wanted to go and say thank you but the security personnel said it would be mayhem and wouldn't let me. So we went back to the hotel instead.

U2's 'Beautiful Day' was already on full whack by the time I got in the team room and it would be heard another hundred times that night. We were actually quite sensible compared to other Ryder Cup parties. On other occasions I have ended up getting terribly drunk and felt awful the following morning.

At about 10 o'clock I went to have a shower and get out of the pink jacket. It was the sensible thing to do because it stopped me having any drinks for about an hour and allowed my liver to rest.

There was no time for food, it was just drink. I was with my good friend Ronan Keating and his wife. We were sitting outside having a great time and some of the guys came over and invited me into the American team room. Theirs was much bigger than ours, with a karaoke machine. Jim Furyk was rapping away to 50 Cent. It was brilliant. This to me was what the Ryder Cup is all about. Our caddies, their caddies, the players and their wives, all letting their hair down. We were there for ninety minutes and the atmosphere was great between the two teams. Tom Lehman again pulled me aside and said some fantastic words to me. That man has true class.

Then somebody dragged me away and told me to go to our team room to be greeted by all the caddies. John Graham, Lee's caddie, Scotchy, had lifted the flag off the 16th green and got all the players to sign it with little notes. They presented it to me and I had to get up and read the messages out – 'Heather would be so proud' and things like that. I stood up and said I can't thank you enough for this. Then I had another little cry and there was one of those uncomfortable silences when nobody knew what to do next. Somebody tried to move things on but I just said, 'No, no, no, no, I'll be with you in just a second,' and I thanked everybody again for all their support. I told them that the present was huge and would be framed and hung in my office as a constant reminder of an unforgettable week. I also told them that the achievements of that week were due to all of us. We'd all done it, together.

We partied on until about half three or four and then it was off to bed.

On the Monday morning I got up, feeling unbelievably fresh, to read such newspaper headlines as 'Golden Boys', 'Heaven Sent', 'Pure Genius', 'Special K' and 'The Cup of Tears'. Put together, I suppose they just about summed up the week. How on earth I was able to read at all is a mystery, given my intake the previous evening and early morning. I had tipped down gallons upon gallons upon gallons of Guinness but hadn't got drunk.

I also discovered that I had been made the bookmakers' favourite to land the BBC Sports Personality of the Year Award. It was rather embarrassing, but it was pointed out to me that being successful through adversity is every bit as worthy of recognition as succeeding when times are not as stressful and heartbreaking as mine had been. If I did offer hope to anybody going through similar circumstances, I would be proud of it. I hadn't thought that I might be serving as a role model, showing that it is possible to emerge through the other side, even when most days contain more dark clouds than sunshine. If people thought I was worthy of being nominated for the award, I was not going to throw their kindness, gratitude and votes in their face by withdrawing, as was erroneously suggested in some places.

We were up bright and early to get our plane, dropping Lee and Laurae off in Doncaster, and taking off again for the return to Farnborough. Chubby came with us and I got home in time to do the school runs.

Monday evening was okay, but on Tuesday, the reality of everything that had happened kicked in – not the elation from the Ryder Cup, but the realisation of everything I had done to get myself ready for it in the time since Heather passed away.

I did what I had to do at the K Club but the week itself certainly wasn't any easier than I had anticipated. I knew my thoughts would frequently wander off to Heather and what she would have been doing had she been there. The day the wives go to the races, and particularly the one when they get pampered in the spa, she would have been involved in all that.

I missed Heather an unbelievable amount during the week, but because I knew she would have wished me to be there, I got my concentration hat on so that I could perform the way she would have wanted me to. Looking back, it was fantastic to be part of a winning team again, and to do it in Ireland was simply the best, but the most satisfaction I got was the knowledge that Heather would have been proud of me.

2006: K CLUB, Dublin, Ireland

EUROPE		UNITED STATES

FOURBALLS – morning

P. Harrington and C. Montgomerie	0	1	T. Woods and J. Furyk (1 hole)
P. Casey and R. Karlsson (halved)	1/2	1/2	JJ Henry and S. Cink (halved)
S. Garcia and J.M. Olazabal (3 and 2)	1	0	B. Wetterich and D. Toms
D. Clarke and L. Westwood (1 hole)	1	0	P. Mickelson and C. DiMarco

FOURSOMES – afternoon

P. Harrington and P. McGinley (halved)	1/2	1/2	C. Campbell and Z. Johnson (halved)
L. Donald and S. Garcia (2 holes)	1	0	T. Woods and J. Furyk
D. Howell and H. Stenson (halved)	1/2	1/2	S. Cink and D. Toms (halved)
C. Montgomerie and L. Westwood (halved)	1/2	1/2	P. Mickelson and C. DiMarco (halved)

FOURBALLS – morning

P. Casey and R. Karlsson (halved)	1/2	1/2	S. Cink and JJ Henry (halved)
S. Garcia and J.M. Olazabal (3 and 2)	1	0	P. Mickelson and C. DiMarco
L. Westwood and D. Clarke (3 and 2)	1	0	T. Woods and J. Furyk
H. Stenson and P. Harrington	0	1	S. Verplank and Z. Johnson (2 and 1)

FOURSOMES – afternoon

S. Garcia and L. Donald (2 and 1)	1	0	P. Mickelson and D. Toms
C. Montgomerie and L. Westwood (halved)	1/2	1/2	C. Campbell and V. Taylor (halved)
P. Casey and D. Howell (5 and 4)	1	0	S. Cink and Z. Johnson
P. Harrington and P. McGinley	0	1	J. Furyk and T. Woods (3 and 2)

SINGLES – Sunday

C. Montgomerie (1 hole)	1	0	D. Toms
S. Garcia	0	1	S. Cink (4 and 3)
P. Casey (2 and 1)	1	0	J. Furyk
R. Karlsson	0	1	T. Woods (3 and 2)
L. Donald (2 and 1)	1	0	C. Campbell
P. McGinley (halved)	1/2	1/2	JJ Henry (halved)
D. Clarke (3 and 2)	1	0	Z. Johnson
H. Stenson (4 and 3)	1	0	V. Taylor
D. Howell (5 and 4)	1	0	B. Wetterich
J.M. Olazabal (2 and 1)	1	0	P. Mickelson
L. Westwood (2 holes)	1	0	C. DiMarco
P. Harrington	0	1	S. Verplank (4 and 3)

18 1/2	**9 1/2**

Victorious captain – **Ian Woosnam**

Samuel Ryder's gold chalice features a figurine of Abe Mitchell on top.

9 | TEAM PROFILES

Turned professional: **2000**   Ryder Cup: **2004, 2006**
Tournament wins: **7**   Record: **won 3, lost 1, halved 2**
World ranking: **17**   2006 match: **won 2, halved 2**

PAUL CASEY   Age: **29**

Paul Casey proved at the K Club that he is entering his prime as a golfer at the highest level. In fact, it was an amazing fortnight for him after he won his biggest title to date, the HSBC World Matchplay Championship, the week before at Wentworth. He earned a nice big cheque for that win, but it sums up what a good guy he is when he said he would rather win the Ryder Cup than the £1 million. As Ian Woosnam said, that shows the commitment to the team from all the players.

Like Luke Donald, Paul was successful on the American college circuit and won all four of his matches in the 1999 Walker Cup before turning professional.

Paul has improved immeasurably over the years and has all the talent that anybody could ever want. He's comfortably one of the two best players in Europe right now. He has always been a player to feed off confidence and when he gets in the groove there is no stopping him. He is fantastically fit, as he showed at Wentworth and the K Club. Who will ever forget his hole in one at the 14th to win his match in the Saturday foursomes? He will be part of Ryder Cup history forever for that shot, and he should be around to play in many more matches to come.

Turned professional: **1990**

Tournament wins: **14**

World ranking: **24**

Ryder Cup: **1997, 1999, 2002, 2004, 2006**

Record: **won 10, lost 7, halved 3**

2006 match: **won 3**

DARREN CLARKE   Age: **38**

Personally, I owe Ian Woosnam a great debt of gratitude for having the courage to pick me, and I hope I repaid him with the points he wanted from me. As I told him, if I didn't think I could benefit or contribute to the team, I wouldn't have accepted the pick. I am just delighted I was able to help. It was an unbelievable team effort, with everyone performing from top to bottom, and it was fantastic to be a part of it. The support I received from the players, the wives, the American team, the American wives, the captains, vice-captains, everyone really, meant so much. The support from the crowd, especially, was very, very touching.

My playing ability is probably in direct correlation to the amount of Guinness consumed. If I had to assess myself, I'd say usually solid, occasionally rubbish, frequently unsure of exactly how I might perform after leaving the practice range and going to the 1st tee, but when I'm playing well, I'm not afraid of anybody. I relish the challenge of playing against the best in the game.

Turned professional: **2001**

Tournament wins: **5**

World ranking: **9**

Ryder Cup: **2004, 2006**

Record: **won 5, lost 1, halved 1**

2006 match: **won 3**

LUKE DONALD   Age: **28**

A lot of people were surprised, not least probably himself, that Luke Donald did not play more than three times in the competition. It shows what strength in depth Ian Woosnam had if he could afford to leave out of the fourballs a player who has been in the top ten in the world for most of the year. Luke responded brilliantly, teaming up with Sergio Garcia, as he did at Oakland Hills, for two wins in the foursomes, and then beating Chad Campbell in the singles to make sure Europe retained the Cup.

Luke seems to have collected his own personal chant with spectators baying 'Loooooooke' at him. He is good friends with Sergio, even though they appear to be such different characters. Luke is from the Bernhard Langer school of hard work, meticulous preparation and superb course management. He and brother Christian, his caddie, have become a good team. Luke has an amazing record in international team competitions, having won seven times and lost just once in two Walker Cup appearances.

He went to Northwestern University in Chicago, where he studied art, and then joined the US PGA Tour, but he came back to Europe in 2004 and won twice to make the Ryder Cup team at Oakland Hills. This year he won the Honda Classic and played with Tiger Woods in the final round of the USPGA Championship at Medinah. It's a thankless task playing against Tiger at the moment but I'm sure it has left Luke hungry for more chances to win Majors. He will continue going up the world rankings to the top.

Turned professional: **1999**

Tournament wins: **15**

World ranking: **8**

Ryder Cup: **1999, 2002, 2004, 2006**

Record: **won 14, lost 4, halved 2**

2006 match: **won 4, lost 1**

SERGIO GARCIA   Age: **26**

Sergio Garcia is the heartbeat of the Ryder Cup team room, an inexhaustible bundle of energy and a joy to be around. He is yet another of the legendary Spaniards to make their mark on this competition. Seve Ballesteros made the Ryder Cup what it is today and formed a terrific partnership with Jose Maria Olazabal. How fitting that Olly should come back into the team this year and play with Sergio. He said playing with Sergio was less exciting than playing with Seve but more relaxing.

It is amazing to think that Sergio has already played in four Ryder Cups and collected one of the best records there is going, percentage-wise. He could end up with the best record of all time. He has won every foursomes match he has played so far and lost only one fourball match. Good partners in the shape of Jesper Parnevik, Lee Westwood, Luke Donald and now Olly must have helped, but even so it is a spectacular achievement.

Make no mistake, Sergio is a proper, world-class player. No one could argue about his talent since he won his club championship at the age of 12. He has consistently been ranked in the world's top ten and has won regularly in both Europe and America. Problems with re-gripping the club and with his putting have had to be overcome, and in the course of that he has matured a lot as a player and a person. He used to have a big loop at the top of his backswing but he worked hard with his father Victor, also a golf professional, and is now one of the straightest drivers in the game. If he could bring the same passion to the Majors that he shows in the Ryder Cup, there would be no stopping him.

Turned professional: **1995**

Tournament wins: **12**

World ranking: **18**

Ryder Cup: **1999, 2002, 2004, 2006**

Record: **won 7, lost 8, halved 2**

2006 match: **lost 4, halved 1**

PADRAIG HARRINGTON   Age: **35**

Forget his points tally at the K Club, Padraig Harrington is the sort of player you wouldn't want to go into a Ryder Cup without. He works so hard, accepted the burden of playing five times and didn't deserve to come out with only half a point. Sometimes that's just how it works out, but it does not reflect what he contributed to the team effort. I know his overwhelming feeling at the end was one of pride because the match had been staged so well and we won in front of such brilliant fans.

Padraig has developed into one of the world's best players and a wonderful ambassador for Ireland. He had a long amateur career, playing in three Walker Cups, while training to be an accountant, but four Ryder Cup appearances show he was right to turn professional. He has admitted he needed to do a lot of work on his game after turning pro, even though he won in Spain in his rookie season. It was another proud day when Padraig and Paul McGinley won the World Cup for Ireland in 1997 at Kiawah Island, thirty-nine years after Harry Bradshaw and Christy O'Connor Senior were victorious in Mexico.

Padraig has a tremendous work ethic, whether on the practice range at Largs with Bob Torrance or in the gym. It has paid off as he has risen up the rankings, and he won twice on the PGA Tour in the States in 2005. Quite how he found the energy to win the Dunhill Links Championship in 2002 just a week after playing in the Ryder Cup I'll never know, although it may have helped that he is teetotal. That said, he has been known to indulge during celebrations at the Ryder Cup, so it's becoming a regular habit!

Turned professional: **1995**

Tournament wins: **5**

World ranking: **13**

Ryder Cup: **2004, 2006**

Record: **won 3, lost 1, halved 1**

2006 match: **won 2, halved 1**

DAVID HOWELL   Age: **31**

David Howell is always great company. He is very witty and his humour is self-deprecating. At the press conference on Sunday night he could not stop saying the phrase, 'pleased as punch'. It became a bit of a theme for the evening, but David was the first to pick up on it and start mocking himself before we could jump on him. A while ago I christened him 'Dangerous Dave' after he handed me an uncomplimentary magazine article to read when those closest to me had been hiding it for a week.

What a fantastic player he has become. Another former Walker Cup man, he had to wait until 1999 for his first win, in Dubai, and then he had to wait even longer for his next. After he won the BMW International in 2005, though, he was on quite a roll. He beat Tiger Woods in a head-to-head battle in China and triumphed at the European Tour's flagship event, the BMW Championship at Wentworth last May. Ernie Els had spent the previous winter tightening up the West course but it didn't seem to make any difference to 'Howeller'. Working with coach Clive Tucker has obviously paid off.

It has to be said that David is a bit accident prone. In 2002 he went jogging, tripped over and broke his arm. Then, in 2005, he picked up Vijay Singh's extra heavy practice club, gave it a couple of swings, pulled a stomach muscle and was out for two months. Even during 2006 he has struggled with the odd injury, otherwise he might have wrapped up the order of merit title ages ago, instead of which Paul Casey and Padraig Harrington helped to make it an exciting race at the end of the season.

Turned professional: **1989**   Ryder Cup: **2006**

Tournament wins: **7**   Record: **lost 1, halved 2**

World ranking: **36**   2006 match: **debut**

ROBERT KARLSSON   Age: 37

Robert Karlsson thoroughly deserved his Ryder Cup debut after just missing out on the team in past years. This has been his most consistent season so far and he can make a ton of birdies when he gets going. He and Paul Casey formed an excellent partnership in the fourballs, and were involved in two great matches against JJ Henry and Stewart Cink. On Sunday, the tall Swede never shied away from the daunting task of taking on Tiger Woods.

Robert may be quiet but he has confidence. You would never imagine that he had thoughts in the past of giving up the game because he was playing poorly. Only two years ago he struggled to keep his card, finishing in last place on the order of merit and narrowly avoiding going back to the Qualifying School. He was so hard on himself and has gone through counselling and psychotherapy to overcome that trait. He has never been afraid of trying something new, including various extreme diets, in his quest to improve.

This summer he won the Wales Open at Celtic Manor and the Deutsche Bank Players Championship of Europe. That was a record seventh victory by a Swede on the European Tour. He almost won the Scandinavian Masters on home soil but lost in a play-off. Being so tall presents its own technical difficulties but he shows superb control with his short irons.

Based in Monaco most of the time, Robert and his family also have a holiday home right at the very top of Sweden, where the sun never sets in the summer but it is dark for three months in the winter. He says it is the most beautiful part of the world and a wonderful place to get away from the golf scene.

Turned professional: **1991**

Tournament wins: **4**

World ranking: **53**

Ryder Cup: **2002, 2004, 2006**

Record: **won 2, lost 2, halved 5**

2006 match: **lost 1, halved 2**

PAUL McGINLEY   Age: **39**

You could not find a better team man than Paul McGinley. Perhaps that's because he started his career in sport playing Gaelic football and turned to golf when he broke his left knee cap at the age of 19. Perhaps it was a lucky break because he will forever be associated with the Ryder Cup. In 2002 at The Belfry he had the honour of holing the winning putt and it was a fantastic moment as he celebrated on the 18th green.

Having played his part in the triumph at Oakland Hills, it would have been such a shame if he had missed out on playing in front of his home crowd in Ireland. He had been struggling for form ever since he had to pull out of the Irish Open in May to have surgery to remove a piece of bone floating in his left knee, a remnant of that earlier operation. He also missed a chance to help secure his place when he pulled out of the USPGA Championship to attend Heather's funeral. So I was personally delighted when he made the team, and he deserved his place as he played brilliantly all week in practice and play. He should have won his singles on Sunday but he is such a gentleman that when a streaker came on the 18th green he did the right thing in conceding JJ Henry's putt.

Paul won the World Cup for Ireland with Padraig Harrington in 1997 but his biggest win as an individual came at the Volvo Masters in 2005 with a brave final-round performance at Valderrama. It was a fitting victory as he had suffered two runner-up finishes earlier in the season at Wentworth in both the BMW Championship and the HSBC World Match Play.

Turned professional: **1987**

Tournament wins: **37**

World ranking: **14**

Ryder Cup: **1991, 1993, 1995, 1997,
1999, 2002, 2004, 2006**

Record: **won 20, lost 9, halved 7**

2006 match: **won 1, lost 1, halved 2**

COLIN MONTGOMERIE   Age: **43**

There is no doubt about it, Colin Montgomerie is a natural born leader in the Ryder Cup. We all want him out there as our number one and he did the job again superbly at the K Club. Just as in 2002 at the Belfry, he made sure there were blue numbers on the scoreboard early on and even though we weren't meant to be looking at the boards, you could tell from the cheers around the course that we were ahead in the early games.

Monty's record in the Ryder Cup is quite phenomenal. He has played eight times and never lost a singles, which is incredible, and overall has earned 23½ points. You wouldn't bet against him coming back in two years' time and trying to beat Nick Faldo's record of 25 points. In 2004 he and Padraig Harrington gave us the perfect start when they beat Tiger Woods and Phil Mickelson in the top match on Friday morning, and Monty went on to hole the winning putt on Sunday. This year he holed a great putt on the 18th green on Friday night to help us extend our lead, and then defeated David Toms for the second match running in the singles.

Every time you come away from a Ryder Cup it is hard to understand why he has not won a Major championship. He has been close so often, especially in the last two seasons, finishing runner-up to Tiger Woods in the Open at St Andrews in 2005 and in the 2006 US Open. He has done everything else in the game, setting a record that may never be beaten in winning seven order of merit titles in a row. He added an eighth for good measure in 2005.

Turned professional: **1985**

Tournament wins: **29**

(including two Majors)

World ranking: **19**

Ryder Cup: **1987, 1989, 1991,
1993, 1997, 1999, 2006**

Record: **won 18, lost 8, halved 5**

2006 match: **won 3**

JOSE MARIA OLAZABAL   Age: **40**

It is hard to believe it was seven years since Jose Maria Olazabal had played in the Ryder Cup. It was a joy to have him back on the team. He is an utter gentleman and he never gives up, even when facing the sternest of tasks. Of course, when he first came in to the Ryder Cup team he was the young cub playing with his hero, Seve Ballesteros. Now he has gone the full circle, playing the elder statesman to Sergio Garcia's gazelle.

Seve and Olly were legendary in the Ryder Cup. They won 11, halved two and lost only two of their matches together. The combination of Olly and Sergio didn't get off to a bad start as they won their two fourball games together. Jose then beat Phil Mickelson in the singles for a clean sweep, and further improved his stellar record in the Cup.

Olly has worked hard on improving his driving in recent years with Butch Harmon, but he will always be remembered for his iron play and his amazing short game, something that is clearly in the Spanish golfing genes. He won the Masters twice, in 1994 and 1999, but the amazing part of the story is that in between he missed over 18 months' golf while suffering from rheumatoid polyarthritis. There were days he could not even get out of bed and he must have feared he would never be able to play golf again. He grew up next to Real Golf Club de San Sebastian, where first his grandfather and then his father were greenkeepers. He beat Colin Montgomerie to win the British Amateur in 1984 and once won the World Series at Firestone by 12 strokes. Having won over the same course, I still find that a mind-boggling achievement.

Turned professional: **1998**   Ryder Cup: **2006**
Tournament wins: **4**   Record: **won 1, lost 1, halved 1**
World ranking: **11**   2006 match: **debut**

HENRIK STENSON   Age: **30**

You never wish anyone to miss a putt – not an opponent, let alone a team-mate – so it is only right and proper that it goes down in history that Henrik Stenson was the player to hole the winning putt at the 2006 Ryder Cup. Of course, if the timing had been slightly different, I might have had that honour, and there again it might have been Luke Donald. Ultimately, the only thing that matters is that the team wins. All you can do when you are out there is concentrate on your own match and that is why Henrik deserves all the credit for making sure he beat Vaughn Taylor so handsomely 4 and 3. He admitted he had no idea it was the winning putt but the point made up for his first two matches, when he was unlucky not to post more than a half.

Henrik is a very strong player. The way he came through a tough spell earlier in his career and then played as he did at the K Club shows there are no real boundaries for him. Like Robert Karlsson, he is another tall Swede, a big hitter with power to spare. He burst on to the scene by winning the Benson and Hedges International in 2001 and there was talk of him being a Ryder Cup player in his rookie season. Perhaps the success came a bit early as he struggled the following year before hooking up with coach Peter Cowen. Since then, he has got better and better. He won again late in 2004 and although 2005 was a barren year with three runners-up finishes, he displayed his undoubted talent in 2006 in winning the Qatar Masters and the BMW International in Munich.

Turned professional: **1993**   Ryder Cup: **1997, 1999, 2002, 2004, 2006**
Tournament wins: **26**   Record: **won 14, lost 8, halved 3**
World ranking: **51**   2006 match: **won 3, halved 2**

LEE WESTWOOD   Age: **33**

Lee Westwood is a fantastic player and an even better friend. I have to say that, otherwise I'll never hear the end of it from him, but it doesn't stop it being the truth. He is magnificent under pressure with the heart of a lion. I could not have been handed a better ally for the fourballs than Lee. We know each other's game so well. He doesn't usually say an awful lot when we are in a match unless I'm misbehaving and losing my head. I managed not to do that at the K Club, so that's probably down to him.

For the second straight match, Lee tied with Sergio Garcia as the top point scorer for Europe. He has a tremendous record in the Ryder Cup going back to when he was paired with Nick Faldo in 1997 at Valderrama. In 2002, when the team had been picked the previous season, Lee was struggling for form but he has the priceless ability to dig deep and produce his best golf when the pressure is really on. That year the captain, Sam Torrance, tried to take the pressure off Lee by splitting up our partnership. Sometimes when you have a track record to maintain it can put the pressure on, but we've proved in the last two matches that we are so comfortable together. Overall, we have won six of our eight matches in the Ryder Cup. Lee went on to win his singles against Chris DiMarco even though the hypochondriac had a raging temperature. His tonsils are shocking but he seems to play his best when he is sick. Best season to date came in 2000 when he won six times and claimed the order of merit title off Monty.

Turned professional: **1982**

Tournament wins: **6 (including one Major)**

World ranking: **39**

Ryder Cup: **1995, 1997, 1999**

Record: **won 5, lost 3, halved 2**

2006 match: **captain**

TOM LEHMAN

Age: **47**

Tom Lehman was everything you would have wanted from a Ryder Cup captain. He was an eloquent spokesman, a natural leader, a considerate manager and a charming guest in a foreign land. He appeared to do everything absolutely right both before and during the match but it didn't seem to make any difference. On this occasion he just came up against a team who played out of their socks. As you would expect, he was very gracious in defeat and, on a personal note, I should add that he was exceptionally kind to me throughout the week.

All Ryder Cup captains work enormously hard throughout the year leading up to the tournament, but it does seem at the moment that it is a more difficult job in America than in Europe. Ian Woosnam had the advantage not just of playing in the Ryder Cup but also being a vice-captain to Sam Torrance. Tom played in three Ryder Cups and although America lost two of those matches, the fact that he came out with a record of 6 points out of 10 shows what a strong opponent he was.

In the singles in 1995 he was playing against Seve Ballesteros in the top match. Seve could not hit a fairway to save his life – Tom is exactly the opposite, a fairways and greens man who perennially challenged at the US Open – but the Spaniard was employing all his legendary recovery skills to stay in the match. Seve was still only one down after 10 holes. A lesser man than Lehman might have cracked but he did not. Tom played a lot around the world before making it on the PGA Tour but his crowning glory came when he won the Open Championship at Royal Lytham and St Annes in 1996.

Turned professional: **1996**

Tournament wins: **3**

World ranking: **22**

Ryder Cup: **2004, 2006**

Record: **won 1, lost 3, halved 2**

2006 match: **lost 1, halved 2**

CHAD CAMPBELL   Age: **32**

Playing in his second Ryder Cup, Chad Campbell was involved in two classic matches in each session of the foursomes. On Friday, Chad and Zach Johnson birdied the last three holes to come from two down to force a half against Padraig Harrington and Paul McGinley. Then, on Saturday, he and Vaughn Taylor shared another half with Colin Montgomerie and Lee Westwood by winning the 17th and matching birdies at the last. After ten holes halved in pars in the singles, Luke Donald ran away with their match as the Englishman gained revenge for Campbell's 5 and 3 victory over him at Oakland Hills.

It was not the Ryder Cup Chad would have wanted but he is a natural player who can play awesome golf when he's right on song. His first win on the PGA Tour came at the Tour Championship in 2003, while he won another top-class event, the Bay Hill Invitational, the following year. This year he added the Bob Hope Chrysler Classic. As a Texan, he is used to playing in the wind and hits the ball lower than some. He has still to find consistent form in the Majors, although he was third at the Masters this year. In 2003 fellow players voted him the newcomer most likely to win a Major in the magazine *Sports Illustrated*. His wife Amy is a highly talented singer with her own professional career.

Turned professional: **1995**

Tournament wins: **6**

World ranking: **23**

Ryder Cup: **2002, 2004, 2006**

Record: **won 3, lost 5, halved 4**

2006 match: **won 1, lost 1, halved 3**

STEWART CINK   Age: **33**

Stewart Cink was always going to be one of Tom Lehman's wild-card picks, even though it was the second time in a row. Stewart totally justified the selection with his immaculate play. He played in all five sessions and gave his all. He was involved in just one defeat, and that was when Paul Casey and David Howell went crazy in the foursomes on Saturday. His first three matches were nerve-wracking affairs that went all the way to the 18th and yet he still had enough energy to come out all guns blazing on Sunday. He played brilliantly, holed everything and never gave the mighty Sergio Garcia a chance as he won 4 and 3. He could not have done anything more yet his was one of too few American points in the singles.

Stewart has won four times on the PGA Tour, including at the NEC Invitational at Firestone in 2004, one of the World Golf Championship events. He almost repeated his victory at Firestone this year in the Bridgestone event but lost to Tiger Woods in a play-off. Stewart took up the game when he was left at a driving range while his parents, single-digit golfers, went off to play. He lives near Atlanta, in Georgia, and is a member of the legendary East Lake club, where Bobby Jones learned the game and which now hosts the US Tour Championship.

Turned professional: **1990**

Tournament wins: **4**

World ranking: **15**

Ryder Cup: **2004, 2006**

Record: **won 2, lost 4, halved 2**

2006 match: **lost 3, halved 1**

CHRIS DiMARCO   Age: **38**

Sadly, Chris DiMarco went through a bereavement this year, so he could empathise with my circumstances. In July his mother, Norma, died suddenly. Yet a few weeks later, with his father Rich watching from outside the ropes, Chris put up a spirited challenge to Tiger Woods at the Open Championship at Hoylake. It was not the first time DiMarco has chased Tiger home, taking him to a play-off before Woods won the Masters in 2005. Chris is a hell of a gritty player and never gives up.

I'm sure he will have wanted to get more out of the Ryder Cup. He arrived as part of a much-vaunted partnership with Phil Mickelson. They had won 3½ points out of 4 together at the President's Cup in 2005, but from the moment they were unlucky enough to come up against Westwood and Clarke on Friday morning, it did not work out for them this time. They claimed just half a point from three matches. Then in the singles, Westwood made life uncomfortable for Chris by birdieing five of the first seven holes.

Chris turned his career around when he converted to the 'claw' putting method. He started 2006 in fine form winning the Abu Dhabi Championship on the European Tour but then suffered a skiing accident and the injury led to a dip in form. It wasn't until the Open that he secured his place on the team, but he should be around again in two years' time.

Turned professional: **1992**

Tournament wins: **14**

(including one Major)

World ranking: **3**

Ryder Cup: **1997, 1999,
2002, 2004, 2006**

Record: **won 6, lost 12, halved 2**

2006 match: **won 2, lost 3**

JIM FURYK   Age: **36**

Jim Furyk is not just a great player but a tenacious one. The first hole of the 2006 Ryder Cup sums him up to a tee. His playing partner, a certain world number one, Tiger Woods, is in the water off the tee, having hooked his drive, and Jim stands up, makes a birdie and wins the hole. There were many times over the first two days when Tiger was struggling with his form and Furyk was the strong man of the partnership. Two wins and two defeats do not represent the effort the pair put in for their team.

On Sunday, Jim was unlucky to meet a rampant Paul Casey. Paul knew he was facing one of the strongest players in the US side, and one who had never lost a singles before. Paul got ahead early on but Jim never backed off and played brilliantly on the inward nine, including an eagle at the 16th, to take the match to the penultimate hole. The pair shared eight birdies and an eagle in eight holes on the back nine. Throughout, Jim looked grimly determined, stony faced and was clearly never going to give up. Don't let his countenance fool you, though. Jim is in the Olazabal mode as a true gentleman of the game.

Jim has one of the most unorthodox swings around today, with a big loop at the top of the backswing, but it repeats every time and he works hard with his father, Mike, who is his only coach. He has putted cross-handed since the age of seven after getting a tip from Arnold Palmer. Jim won the Canadian Open just before the Ryder Cup for his twelfth win on the PGA Tour, but the highlight of his career came when he won the US Open at Olympia Fields in 2003.

Turned professional: **1998**
Tournament wins: **1**
World ranking: **64**

Ryder Cup: **2006**
Record: **halved 3**
2006 match: **debut**

JJ HENRY   Age: **31**

One of four rookies on the American team, JJ Henry may not have been well known to golf fans before he arrived but he certainly is now, after his performance at the K Club. Although he was playing in the tournament for the first time, he looked as if he had been a member of the team for ever, and a long Ryder Cup career seems assured. He comfortably made his way on to the team and performed so courageously, not losing any of his three matches.

The two fourballs he and Stewart Cink played against Paul Casey and Robert Karlsson were classics. In both matches the Americans found themselves down early on but then rallied. On Friday, JJ – he was christened Ronald but has always been known by the family nickname – made a flurry of birdies, while on Saturday he eagled the 16th and birdied the 17th to take the match to the last. He enjoyed another tough encounter in the singles against Paul McGinley and took it all the way to the 18th before Paul conceded a half after the antics of a streaker.

JJ Henry has been on the US Tour since 2001 but won his maiden victory in fairy-tale circumstances in 2006. Although he now lives in Texas, he grew up in Fairfield, Connecticut, and had attended the local PGA Tour event, the Buick Championship, since he was five years old. His father was a good enough golfer to play in the US Amateur Championship and the British Amateur Championship many times. This season at River Highlands he cruised to a 3-stroke victory over Hunter Mahan and Ryan Moore to become the first player from the state to win the event in its fifty-five-year history.

Turned professional: **1998**

Tournament wins: **1**

World ranking: **42**

Ryder Cup: **2006**

Record: **won 1, lost 2, halved 1**

2006 match: **debut**

ZACH JOHNSON   Age: **30**

Unfortunately, Zach Johnson had the golfing gods against him in the singles on Sunday when he was drawn against me. Conceding the putt that effectively ended our match at the 16th showed what a true gentleman he is. Obviously, it is an afternoon I'll never forget but from the nice things Zach said afterwards it seemed to be an experience he savoured as well, despite the result. I am sure he enjoyed his week and deservedly so. He was another of the American rookies to have a terrific debut. He came off the bench to play in the foursomes on Friday afternoon and he and Chad Campbell grabbed a half against Ireland's own Padraig Harrington and Paul McGinley.

It was in the fourballs on Saturday morning that he showed what a fine player he is by almost single-handedly beating Harrington and Henrik Stenson, ending the match by chipping in at the 17th. In the afternoon foursomes he had a dose of his own medicine when he and Stewart Cink were blitzed by Paul Casey and David Howell.

Zach showed good head-to-head form earlier in the year at the Accenture World Matchplay when he beat Jim Furyk and Retief Goosen on the way to the semi-finals and then defeated his captain-to-be Tom Lehman in the third/fourth place play-off. He came off the Nationwide Tour to win the BellSouth Classic in his rookie season of 2004, and finished runner-up in the same event in 2006, as well as at the Memorial to book his place on the team.

Turned professional: **1992**

Tournament wins: **29**

(including three Majors)

World ranking: **2**

Ryder Cup: **1995, 1997, 1999, 2002, 2004, 2006**

Record: **won 9, lost 12, halved 4**

2006 match: **lost 4, halved 1**

PHIL MICKELSON   Age: **36**

Talented is too polite a word for the qualities Phil Mickelson possesses as a player. It was obvious he had that in abundance from the moment he won for the first time on the US Tour in 1991 when he was still at college and an amateur. Naturally right-handed, he learned to play left-handed as a mirror image of his father's swing. He has always shown imagination and creativity – his instincts are to pull off the inspirational shot – but he also displays terrific dedication. Phil puts in hours of practice for the Major championships with his coach, Rick Smith, and the short-game guru, Dave Peltz.

It has paid off because he has won a Major in each of the last three years. He won the Masters for the first time in 2004 after an epic duel with Ernie Els and then got the USPGA Championship in 2005 before winning the Masters again last April. The week before, he had lapped the field at the BellSouth Classic and during that fortnight employed the innovative strategy of using two drivers, one for a controlled fade, the other for a powerful draw. He should have won the US Open at Winged Foot but was scuppered by a disastrous double bogey at the 72nd hole.

Phil first played in the Ryder Cup in 1995, when he won all three of his matches, and his record was superb until the last couple of matches. Obviously, things did not go his way at the K Club as his partnership with Chris DiMarco, so successful in the 2005 President's Cup, failed to get going this time. Typically, as a devoted family man, he showed a lot of compassion for me throughout the Ryder Cup, which is something I will never forget.

Turned professional: **1999**

Tournament wins: **2**

World ranking: **60**

Ryder Cup: **2006**

Record: **lost 1, halved 1**

2006 match: **debut**

VAUGHN TAYLOR   Age: **30**

He may be quiet and reserved but Vaughn Taylor is a gritty character who will have benefited from the experience of playing in his first Ryder Cup. This is only his third full season on the PGA Tour and clearly his most important to date. He won the Reno-Tahoe Open in his rookie year in 2004 and then, even more impressively, he defended the title successfully the following year.

This year he had a number of significant top-ten finishes to secure his place on the team but his biggest moment in golf prior to playing in the Ryder Cup came at the Masters. Vaughn grew up in Augusta, Georgia, and his family has attended the Masters every year. This year he became the first Augusta resident for fifty years to play in the Masters and said he had never been so nervous on the 1st tee – but he did hit it straight down the middle.

Vaughn was required to sit out the first day and a half at the K Club but stepped in bravely to partner Chad Campbell to a half in the foursomes against Colin Montgomerie and Lee Westwood. Vaughn has a great short game but in the singles was unable to prevent Henrik Stenson posting the winning point.

Turned professional: **1989**

Tournament wins: **13**

(including one Major)

World ranking: **16**

Ryder Cup: **2002, 2004, 2006**

Record: **won 4, lost 6, halved 2**

2006 match: **lost 3, halved 1**

DAVID TOMS   Age: **39**

Another rock-solid player, David Toms played excellently all week but did not get the results his performances deserved. He was not helped by playing with a different partner in each of his first three matches and then coming up against the indomitable Colin Montgomerie in the singles. David was unable to get his revenge for defeat by Monty in 2004 at Oakland Hills. As his Ryder Cup debut at The Belfry in 2002 showed, he is a tenacious opponent in matchplay. He won 3½ points out of 4 and defeated Sergio Garcia on the final day for one of the rare American highlights on that Sunday.

David has won twelve times on the PGA Tour dating back to 1997, including the Accenture World Matchplay in 2005 and the Sony Open in Hawaii at the start of 2006. The highlight of his career came when he won the USPGA Championship in 2001 at the Atlanta Athletic Club. He holed in one during the third round and held off the challenge of Phil Mickelson on the last day. At the final hole, he was forced to lay up in front of the water by the green but then got up and down to clinch victory.

Based in Shreveport, Louisiana, David established a children's foundation in 2003, which helped to raise over $1 million for those affected by Hurricane Katrina in 2005.

Turned professional: **1986**
Tournament wins: **4**
World ranking: **37**

Ryder Cup: **2002, 2006**
Record: **won 4, lost 1**
2006 match: **won 2**

SCOTT VERPLANK   Age: **42**

Scott Verplank was a wild-card selection for the second time, after making his debut in 2002. He is a good friend of mine and I am sure he would have liked to play more. Scott performed with great distinction to win two matches out of two. All he had to do in the fourballs on Saturday morning was let Zach Johnson off the leash and let his partner do the damage, but he was in fine form in the singles.

His victory over Padraig Harrington included the second hole in one of the week at the 14th, and the first by an American in the history of the Ryder Cup. Now he has the distinction of winning four of the five matches he has played in two Ryder Cups. His victims include Thomas Bjorn and me in foursomes at the Belfry, and Lee Westwood in the singles. There can be some pressure on the guys who are the wild cards to justify the pick, but Scott doesn't seem to have a problem with that. You could not rule out that he will be picked again.

A Texan who now lives in Oklahoma, Scott won the US Amateur in 1984 and, like Phil Mickelson, he won on the US Tour while still an amateur. His career has been solid rather than spectacular, although he was once labelled as the next best thing. He suffers from diabetes and has twice had surgery on his elbow.

BRETT WETTERICH

Turned professional: **1994**

Tournament wins: **1**

World ranking: **68**

Ryder Cup: **2006**

Record: **lost 2**

2006 match: **debut**

Elin and Tiger Woods arrive for the welcome dinner. I was pleased the organisers had put me next to them at dinner because we had time for a good old chat.

An emotional reception greets me at the gala dinner. Passing that test was another tiny, yet significant, step.

Amy Mickelson (*third from the right*) made the exit from the opening ceremony easier by linking arms – a wonderful gesture.

A 'hare'-raising week – probably just saw a Tiger.

Jim Furyk and Tiger Woods practise their synchronised putting.

A group of magicians, otherwise known as the European Ryder Cup team, assemble for the gala dinner.

Left: Tiger Woods hits his opening tee shot into the water – not what the best player in the world wanted to see but reassuring for the rest of us.

Below left: Keeping my focus at the scenic 14th green.

Right: To be out there, to play well and to win a point with Lee on the first morning was a huge relief.

Below: The new Seve and Olly – Sergio Garcia and Jose Maria Olazabal combined brilliantly for Europe's first point on Friday morning.

Left: Luke Donald sat out the fourballs but showed he was on form in the afternoon foursomes.

Below: Donald and Garcia, reserved Englishman and excitable Spaniard, are good friends and make a winning combination, as Tiger Woods and Jim Furyk found out in Friday's foursomes.

Friend and travelling companion, Lee Westwood is a fantastic player with the heart of a lion – you could not ask for a better partner.

It is always thrilling to beat the best player in the game but Tiger is never less than gracious in defeat.

Celebrating with Lee Westwood and Billy Foster (*right*) after chipping in on the 16th to beat Tiger Woods and Jim Furyk on Saturday.

What a way to end a match! Paul Casey holes in one at the 14th to give him and David Howell victory over Stewart Cink and Zach Johnson on Saturday afternoon.

Caddie Steve Williams slips and drops Tiger Woods' nine iron into the pond at the 7th hole. It had to be retrieved by frogmen.

Stewart Cink was in full flow on Sunday, and not even Sergio Garcia could stop him.

Jim Furyk battled hard during his singles but Paul Casey scored an important win for us.

Tiger Woods, back to his best, claims another point for America in the singles.

Luke Donald defeats Chad Campbell at the 17th by holing the putt that ensures Europe retain the Ryder Cup.

Moments before my match finishes, Henrik Stenson holes the putt that wins the Ryder Cup for Europe. I wasn't fazed – it was fantastic for Henrik.

A birdie at the 4th gives me an early lead over Zach Johnson in the singles.

Billy couldn't believe it when I holed a monster putt at the 12th against Zach Johnson in the singles – nor could I.

The floodgates open after winning my singles. 'It's destiny,' says Ian Woosnam.

Paul McGinley offers a half to JJ Henry after a streaker intervenes.

Chris DiMarco concedes defeat at the 18th to Lee Westwood, who maintained his unbeaten run from Detroit two years ago.

Players and caddies look on at the 16th as my singles comes to a conclusion.

Padraig Harrington, Paul McGinley and I celebrate a Ryder Cup victory on Irish soil.

Downing a pint of Guinness on the clubhouse balcony was not a problem – it would have been rude not to.

Lee Westwood gets the shampoo treatment at the 18th green.

BRETT WETTERICH   Age: **33**

Brett Wetterich was the fourth of the American rookies and very underrated by people who didn't know him. I think he is destined to go further. He hits the ball an absolute mile – he averages almost 310 yards off the tee on the PGA Tour – and is one of the best ball-strikers around. This year has been huge for Brett. In 2005 he finished 132nd on the money list and had to go back to the Qualifying School, but this year his game has come together and he won his maiden title at the Byron Nelson Championship in Dallas. It was a quality performance as he came back on the final day to beat Trevor Immelman and Adam Scott and justified his place on the American team. Like all the rookies, he will benefit from having been around Tiger Woods and Phil Mickelson. He and David Toms were unfortunate in the fourballs on Friday to come up against the inspired pairing of Sergio Garcia and Jose Maria Olazabal, and when Brett next teed up, in the singles, he found David Howell in birdie mode.

Brett was introduced to the game by his father at the age of two and has had to overcome some adversity. During his rookie year on the US Tour, 2000, he injured his wrist and missed most of the season. Then three years ago, his brother Mark was killed in a car accident by a drunk-driver in Chicago. He still carries the initials 'MTW' on his golf bag.

Turned professional: **1996**

Tournament wins: **64**

(including 12 Majors)

World ranking: **1**

Ryder Cup: **1997, 1999, 2002,**
2004, 2006

Record: **won 10, lost 13, halved 2**

2006 match: **won 3, lost 2**

TIGER WOODS
Age: **30**

Simply the best, as a golfer and a person – nothing sums up Tiger Woods better for me. We have been good friends for a while but have become much closer this year. His support both before and during the Ryder Cup is something I appreciate so much. More than ever this year, we have hardly talked about golf. I know how much his father meant to him and how he was affected when Earl passed away in May. Tiger came back at the US Open and missed the cut in a Major for the first time in his professional career. When he won the Open Championship at Hoylake we could all see how emotional he was and his run of victories afterwards was simply astonishing. His win at the USPGA Championship brought his Major tally to 12 and surely Jack Nicklaus's record of 18 is within his grasp.

If there is one area of the game where he has not had the results he has wanted it is in the Ryder Cup. At the K Club he struggled at times with his game. He was just that little bit out of sync, couldn't get his timing exactly right, and wasn't making any putts. It happens to everyone but Tiger's standards are so high, and everyone's expectations of him are so high, that it is highlighted all the more. However, he is such a terrific competitor, and he had a great partner in Jim Furyk, that at the end of the week he ended up with 3 points out of 5, the best of the US side. You certainly can't fault his commitment to the cause.

Personally, I have always relished playing against Tiger. If you can't learn from playing against the best, there is something wrong. Beating him in the final of the Accenture World Matchplay in 2000 remains one of my best achievements, but his friendship means even more to me.

The 18th hole at the K Club presents a dramatic vista.

10 | HOLE-BY-HOLE GUIDE

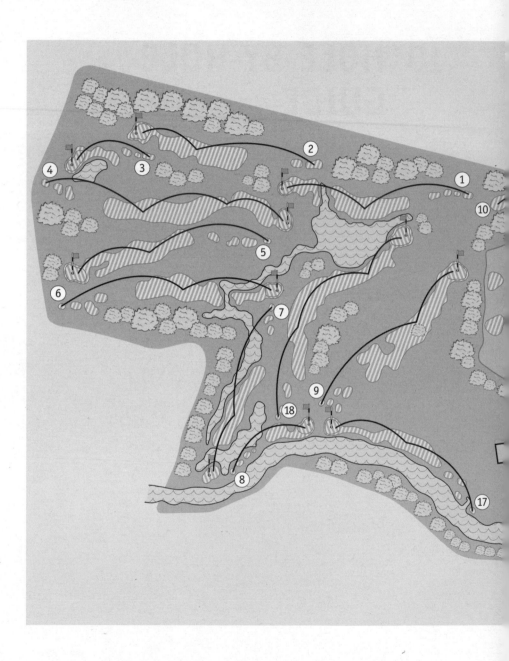

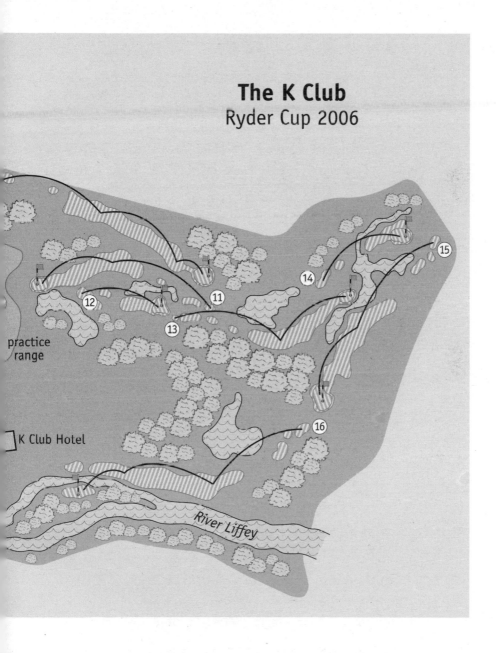

The K Club
Ryder Cup 2006

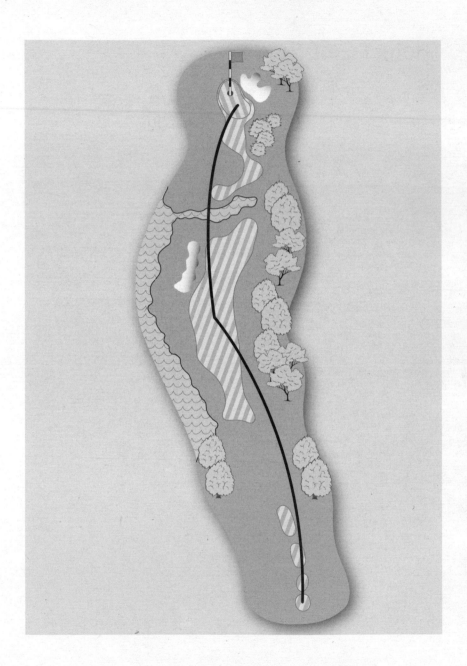

Hole 1 | **BOHEREEN ROAD**

Par 4

418 yards

Even Tiger Woods is not immune from 1st-tee nerves at the Ryder Cup. His opening strike, with a four wood, sailed well left into the lake by the 18th green. The water should not have been in play but the bunker up on the left at 265 yards certainly was as players tried to stay out of the trees on the right, some planted especially for the event by European captain Ian Woosnam. Fortunately for Tiger, he landed in the water in the opening fourballs and partner Jim Furyk bailed him out with a birdie. I hit a momentous drive on Friday for an opening birdie while in the Saturday fourballs Furyk and Lee Westwood combined to halve the hole in 3s. Neither side had an advantage here, each winning the first hole six times.

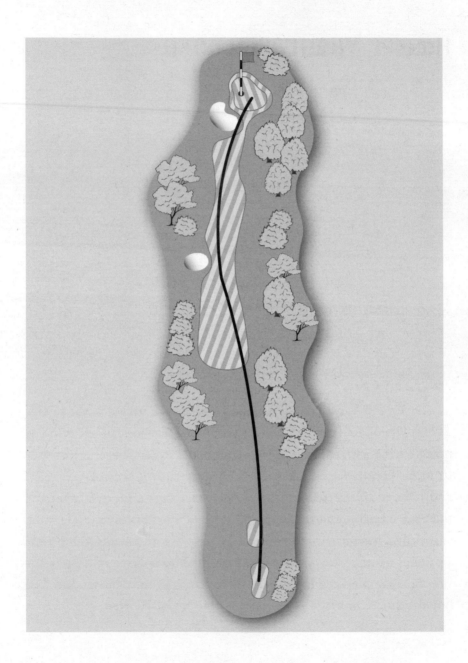

Hole 2 | **THE TUNNEL**

Par 4

413 yards

This is where Europe's dominance of the opening holes began. We posted more wins than our opponents did at all but one of the holes from the 2nd to the 8th. At the straight, and fairly straightforward, 2nd hole, we claimed eight wins to America's five. As at the first, there is one bunker to avoid on the left at 270 yards, and an aggressive drive leaves a wedge to the green, which is protected by a bunker front-left. David Toms made a brave 3 here in the Friday fourballs to prevent going two down after Jose Maria Olazabal holed from 12 feet to follow Sergio Garcia's birdie at the first.

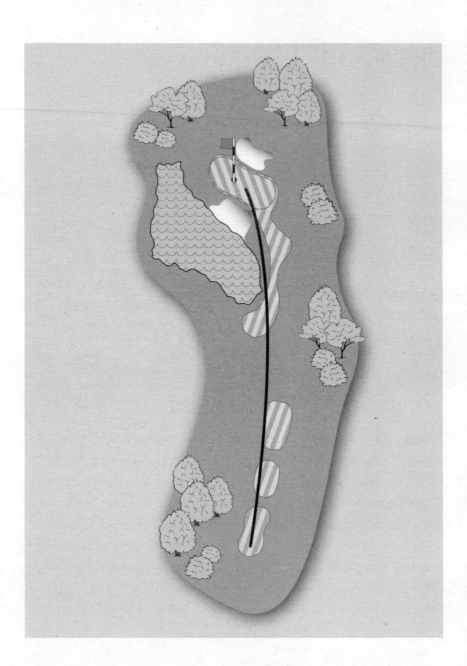

Hole 3 | **THE ISLAND BEACH**

Par 3

170 yards

The first short hole of the round, the 3rd has a shallow green that makes club selection difficult in the wind. There are bunkers front and back, and the water, short of the front bunker, was in play. A ridge across the green divides the putting surface into two distinct sections. Europe won this hole nine times against three wins by the Americans. That may have been due to our greater experience of the course, derived from years of playing in the Smurfit European Open at the K Club. Padraig Harrington holed from 14 feet in the Saturday foursomes for a half after Tiger Woods had made his birdie from 18 feet. Lee Westwood and Chris DiMarco also halved the hole in birdie 2s on Sunday.

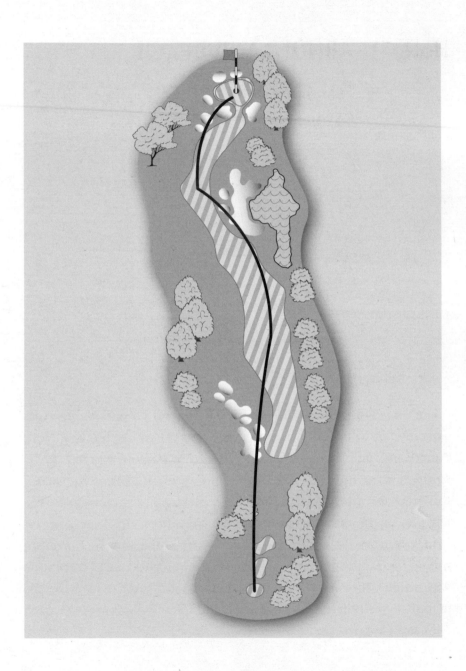

Hole 4 | **ARNOLD'S PICK**

Par 5
568 yards

This hole is named after course designer Arnold Palmer, and the Americans could have done with some of the great man's attacking spirit. It was the home side that were again more comfortable on this reachable par 5. A 300-yard plus drive over the mounds on the left sets up the line to the green. Paul Casey set the tone in the Friday morning fourballs by hitting a three wood to eight feet and holing the putt for the only eagle of the week at the hole. A birdie was no guarantee of a win in the fourballs but it was a different matter in the foursomes. Europe won the hole 12 times while the Americans won it six times.

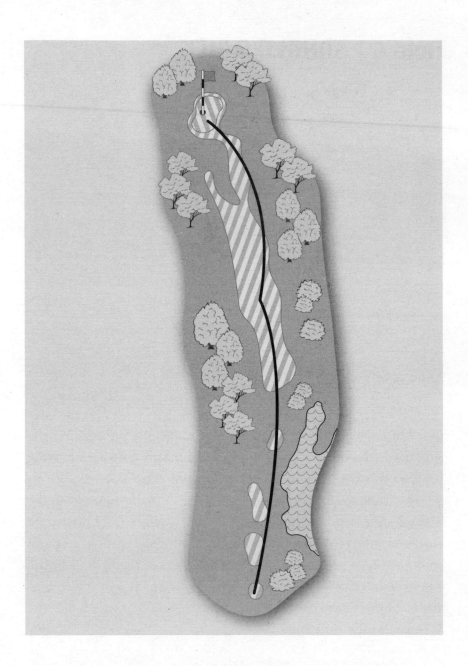

Hole 5 | SQUARE MEADOW

Par 4
440 yards

A medium length par 4, this hole has a tricky approach shot as the green is perched on a hill and runs away from the player. For the tee shot, most players favour a draw as a swale on the right helps to protect the green. For the first time, there was evidence of some resistance from the visitors as the Americans won the hole nine times to our five. Zach Johnson and Padraig Harrington extended their private battle by halving the hole in birdies for the third hole out of four. In the singles, Stewart Cink posted his fourth birdie of the round here as he won six of the first seven holes against Sergio Garcia.

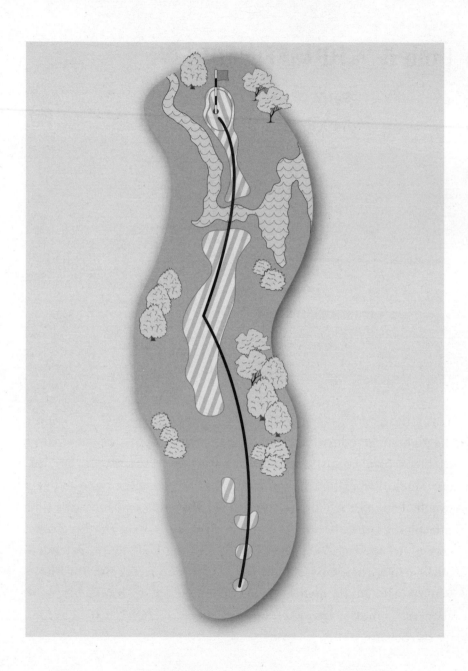

Hole 6 | **THE LIFFEY STREAM**

Par 4

478 yards

This long par 4 is a difficult driving hole. There is more room down the right than you first think, but driving too far right leaves a trickier second shot. The key is to find the fairway, because there is too much danger lurking for an uncontrolled approach from the rough. The stream cuts the fairway and then runs up the left-hand side of the green. Par here is a good score and was often good enough to win the hole. Once it was halved in bogeys and once in birdies, Sergio Garcia holing from 20 feet in the Friday fourballs when both his opponents, David Toms and Brett Wetterich, had chances. Toms converted for the half. The hole was won nine times by Europeans, four times by Americans.

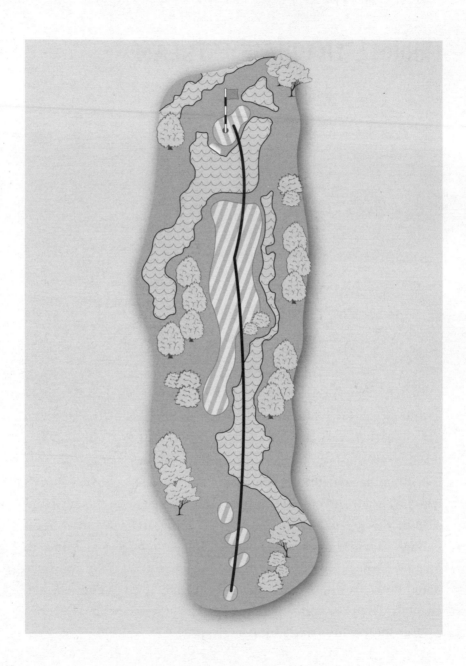

Hole 7 | **MICHAEL'S FAVOURITE**

Par 4
430 yards

Michael Smurfit, the owner of the K Club, obviously knows the course well, and the 7th was a scene of drama throughout the Ryder Cup. The drive has to fit between the trees on the left and the creek on the right, but the pond in front of the green, which protects two and a half sides of the putting surface, is the biggest danger. Zach Johnson found water twice in the singles, off the tee and short of the green. Robert Karlsson, ordered by captain Ian Woosnam not to be short, hit his approach on top of a television camera tower in the Friday fourballs, but after a free drop, got up and down to win the hole. Tiger Woods' nine iron ended up in the pond, dropped by his caddie. Europeans had nine wins here to three by Americans.

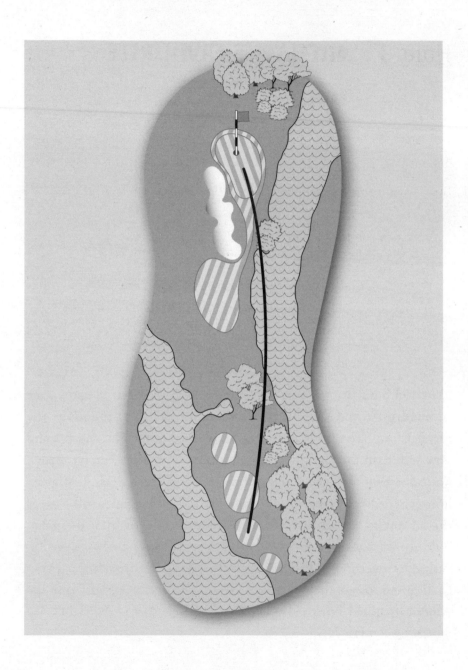

Hole 8 | MAYFLY CORNER

Par 3

173 yards

In this attractive corner of the course, the green slopes left to right towards the River Liffey. The difficulty of the hole depends a lot on wind direction and playing conditions, which is why there may not have been as many birdies at the 8th as some expected. The hole was exchanged seven times, but again the home side had the advantage, coming out on top five times. Nothing went quite right for Phil Mickelson here. He hit his tee shot to four feet in the Saturday foursomes but Luke Donald holed a putt from the edge of the green for a half in birdies. Then in the singles, the left-handed American holed from 30 feet only for Jose Maria Olazabal to match his 2 with an 18-footer.

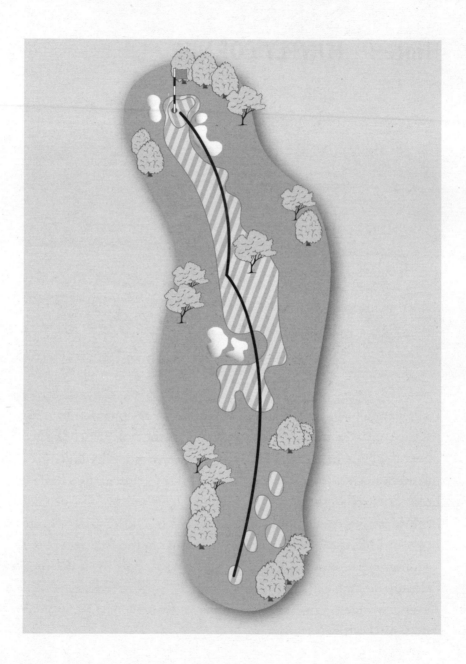

Hole 9 | THE EYE OF THE NEEDLE

Par 4

461 yards

The magnificent tree in the middle of the fairway, 280 yards from the tee, is the main feature of this hole. The drive has to be threaded over the fairway bunkers on the left at 230 yards and past the left-hand side of the tree. The danger at the green is going over the back and down the slope. Padraig Harrington did just that in the Saturday foursomes and handed Tiger Woods and Jim Furyk their two-up lead back. Earlier on the same afternoon, however, Colin Montgomerie chipped in for a half when Vaughn Taylor had already holed from 25 feet for a 3. This was the second hole on the front nine that was won more often by the visitors than by the home side, six times to five.

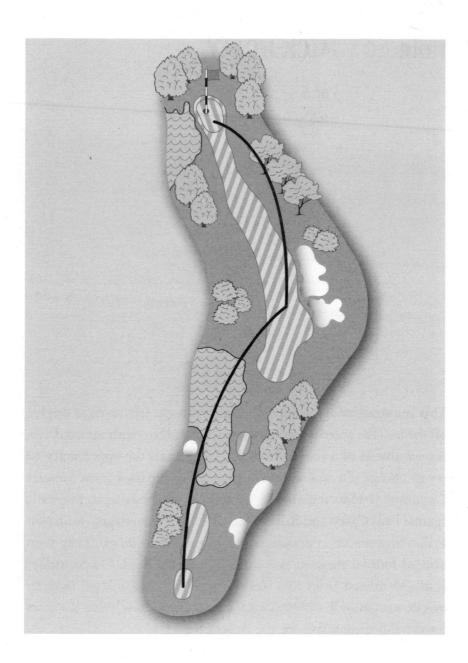

Hole 11 | **LILY POND**

Par 4
415 yards

In the fourballs, players had to be thinking birdie at this classic risk-and-reward hole, but par won it more than once in the foursomes. The hole doglegs sharply to the left and a 300-yard drive over the corner leaves a wedge to the green. Miss the fairway, however, and there's a problem. The second shot taken from the rough is harder to control, and a ball landing on the left half of the green is liable to run into the water. Luke Donald and Chad Campbell had halved the first ten holes in pars in the singles before Luke holed a 30-footer at the 11th, winning the first of three holes in a row. David Howell's chip-in 3 here on Sunday was the first of four wins in a row, a run that saw off Brett Wetterich. However, overall the US took this hole six times to Europe's five.

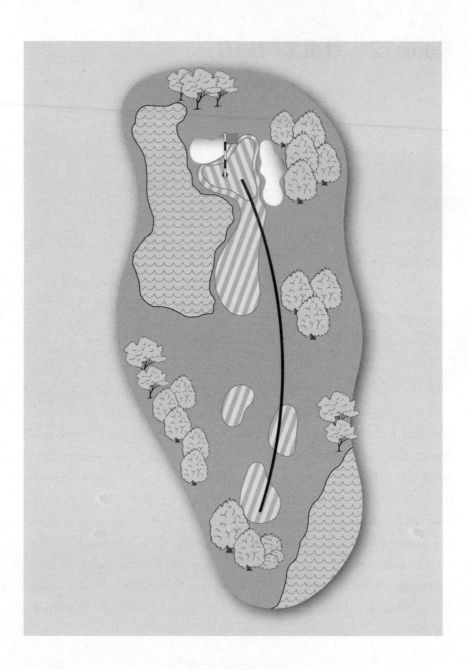

Hole 12 | **THE DOMAIN**

Par 3

182 yards

The three-cornered green is defended by bunkers right and back-left, and by a pond short and left. Find the wrong portion of the green and it is usually a difficult 2-putt. This was not the case for me in the singles on Sunday, though, when I holed a monster across the green from 150 feet for a 2 against Zach Johnson. This short hole was the scene of fluctuating fortunes, with Europe winning the hole nine times and America six times. Tiger Woods and JJ Henry chalked up the first two birdies at the hole on Friday morning but after that it was kinder to the home side. Phil Mickelson found the water on Sunday but Jose Maria Olazabal holed from 12 feet anyway for the win.

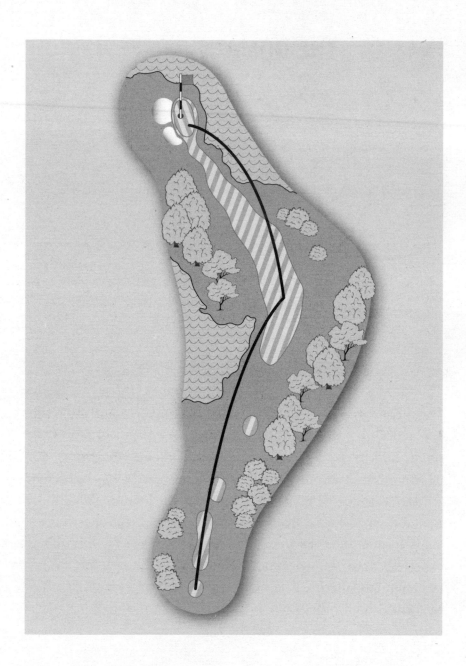

Hole 13 | **LAUREL HAVEN**

Par 4

428 yards

This hole, a medium length par 4, has a sharp dogleg left at 250 yards. The green is defended by water on the right and by two bunkers on the left. A drive over the corner of the dogleg leaves a short-iron approach, but the hole never played as easily as expected. Birdies were scarce and, most surprisingly, there were only two in the fourballs. Both came as Chris DiMarco and I kept our Friday morning match all square with a pair of 3s. The hole gave no advantage to either side as both won it five times.

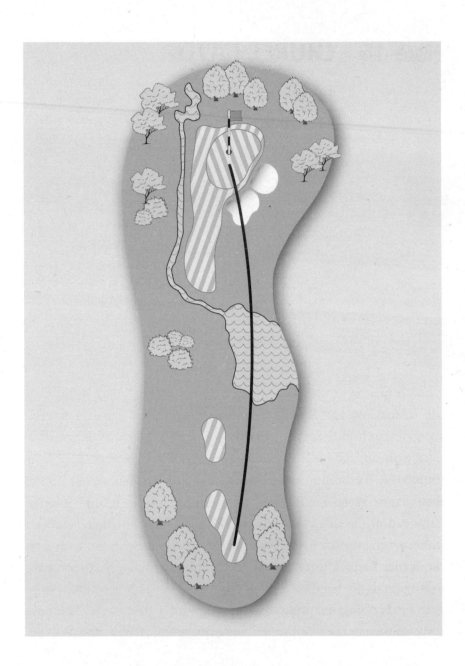

Hole 14 | CHURCH FIELDS

Par 3

213 yards

Church Fields was the scene of the most amazing end to a match in the history of the Ryder Cup. On a day when many players struggled to find the green at this strong par 3, Paul Casey struck a four iron and his ball bounced just short of the hole and then toppled in. As he and David Howell were already dormie five up in their Saturday foursomes, Americans Zach Johnson and Stewart Cink did not even have a chance at the half and could only shake their opponents' hands on the tee. That was the fifth hole in one in the Ryder Cup. The sixth, and the first by an American, came the following day when Scott Verplank repeated the feat. In response, Padraig Harrington drove to 11 feet, which was one of his best shots of the round. As at the 13th, there were five wins apiece here.

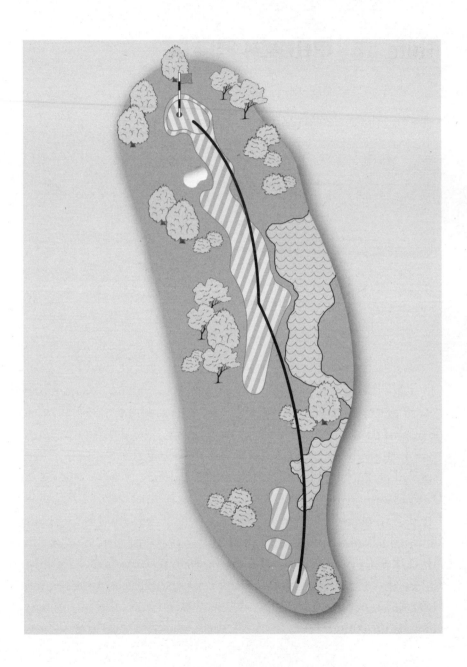

Hole 15 | **PHEASANT RUN**

Par 4

446 yards

Here it was that Henrik Stenson defeated Vaughn Taylor, with a par, and confirmed victory for Europe. At this deceptively strong par 4, the wind comes off the left, bringing the water on the right into play, and a number of players splashed their drives here. The second shot plays uphill, making the bunker that lies 30 yards short of the green on the left an effective guard for the foreshortened approach. There were some important home wins here but, in fact, the US players won more often, six to four. Sergio Garcia, making a late charge for respectability in his singles against Stewart Cink, holed a monster putt here for a 3, but Cink made his 20-footer and clinched a 4 and 3 win.

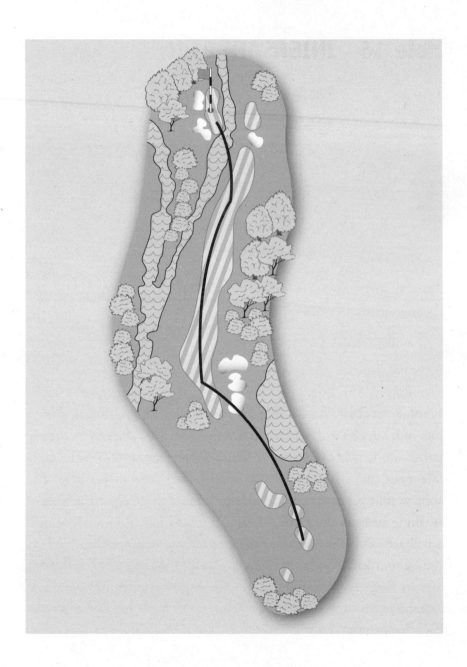

Hole 16 | **INISH MORE**

Par 5

555 yards

A wonderful matchplay hole, and a classic par 5, Inish More has been dubbed the 'greatest in Ireland'. It features a double dogleg. A tributary of the River Liffey runs down the left-hand side and then cuts in front of the green, forcing a decision over whether to attack the green in two or lay up. A huge grandstand on the right-hand side made this a fantastic vantage point. The Americans owned the hole, winning it seven times to Europe's five. JJ Henry on Saturday morning and Jim Furyk on Sunday both had eagles here. However, it will always be associated with Europe's victory, thanks to Sergio Garcia and Jose Maria Olazabal's first win on Friday, my chip-in to win Saturday's fourball, Luke Donald's putt in the Saturday foursomes and the emotional celebrations following my win over Zach Johnson in the singles.

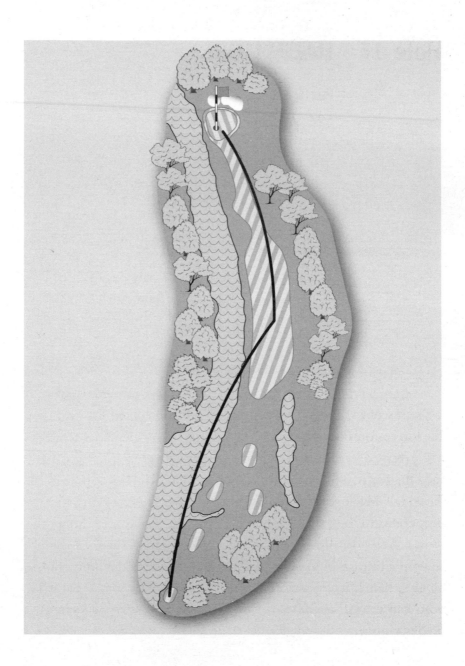

Hole 17 | **HALF MOON**

Par 4
424 yards

This crescent-shaped hole runs along the banks of the River Liffey. New trees on the right block the bail-out shot, making the initial drive very demanding. Thomas Bjorn infamously hit three balls into the water on the way to an 11 in the Smurfit European Open. The Half Moon was another hole that illustrated the Americans' desperate attempts to steal something from their matches, and they won it five times, losing it just twice. Zach Johnson chipped in to sew up a fourball win on Saturday morning but it was here, in the singles, that Luke Donald clinched his win over Chad Campbell, who had visited the Liffey, to make sure Europe would retain the Ryder Cup.

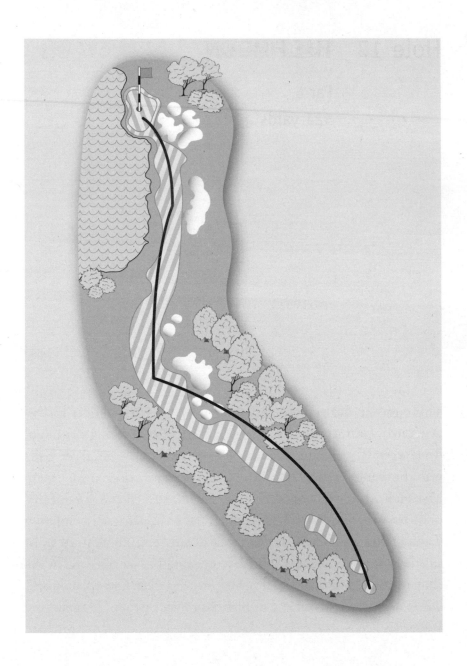

Hole 18 | THE HOOKER'S GRAVEYARD

Par 5
537 yards

The fairway turns sharply to the right, and a drive over the corner of the dogleg requires the ball to carry for more than 300 yards over the bunkers. Then, for the approach shot, the lake at the front and to the left of the green is the key element. This hole has always generated great drama and it was no different at the Ryder Cup. Twelve matches went all the way to the home hole – including eight of the first nine – but America won just one of them, the very first on Friday. The hole was won four times by Europe and only once by America, while it was halved in birdie 4s six times. Chad Campbell and Zach Johnson won the 18th in the Friday foursomes to snatch a half, but in the same session Jim Furyk hit his second shot into the water and then Colin Montgomerie ended the first day with a six-footer for a crucial half point to extend Europe's lead.

Jack Nicklaus and Tony Jacklin share the most famous concession in the history of the Ryder Cup, Royal Birkdale, 1969.

11 | BRIEF HISTORY OF THE RYDER CUP 1927–2006

'What a wonderful day it has been. We must do this again.' So said Samuel Ryder, or words to that effect. How often has such a phrase been used in the clubhouse bar at the end of an excellent day's golf? The sentiment is not always put into action but Ryder was a man of his word. The occasion, at Wentworth in 1926, was an unofficial match between the professionals of Great Britain and a nominal American side that contained a few 'guests' to make up the numbers. This was the second time such a match had taken place, an earlier contest having been played at Gleneagles in 1921.

In 1926, the Americans had come over for the Open Championship at Royal Lytham and St Annes but first there was the little matter of a qualifying tournament at Sunningdale. This was the first time regional qualifying rounds had been deemed necessary, and even the eventual Open champion, the great amateur Bobby Jones, was required to play. The Americans had arrived in Britain earlier than they would otherwise have done and, with time on their hands, agreed to take part in the friendly match at Wentworth, which was won handsomely by the home team.

There is some confusion in the records about whether Ryder had put up the idea of a trophy to be played for on a regular basis before or after the Wentworth match. Whatever the truth may be, the gold chalice with the figurine of Abe Mitchell on top, which cost £250 from silversmiths Mappin and Webb, was first displayed in 1927 at Verulam Golf Club, St Albans. The British team had gathered there for a day's golf before leaving for America for the inaugural match.

Ryder had not taken up golf until after his 50th birthday. The son of a corn merchant from Lancashire, Ryder settled in St Albans in 1895 and set up a mail-order seed company. He thought that long rows of terraced houses, such as the ones where he had grown up, needed brightening up, and his idea was to sell packets of seeds for a penny. It was a brilliant success. Anyone with the tiniest patch of earth could populate it with flowers of many colours, or grow their own vegetables.

Ryder worked tirelessly on the city council, becoming mayor in 1905. He was also a magistrate, a church deacon and a volunteer. It was when his health failed that a friend, the Reverend Frank Wheeler, told him golf would provide the ideal exercise. He took to the hobby so enthusiastically that within a year he had joined the Verulam club with a handicap of six and a year later he was the club captain.

It was entirely within his nature to start sponsoring tournaments and arranging exhibitions at the club. In the early 1920s, he met Abe Mitchell, then the club professional at North Foreland in Kent, and engaged him as his personal professional. The arrangement did not just suit Ryder. It allowed Mitchell the time and money to go off and play all the tournaments, although he never became the Open champion as both men hoped.

Mitchell reported the enthusiasm for a transatlantic match, not just among the British professionals but also the Americans, including Walter Hagen. With the first official match set for Worcester Country Club, in Massachusetts, in 1927, *Golf Illustrated* magazine organised a subscription to send the British team to America. Just as they were due to sail, Mitchell was struck down with appendicitis. It was a bad omen. The passage was rough and, after being wined and dined in the new world, the British team lost by nine matches to two, with one halved.

Ted Ray, who was appointed captain in Mitchell's place, summed up the difference between the teams in a cable to the *Daily Express*. 'Our opponents beat us fairly and squarely,' he said, 'and almost entirely through their astonishing work on the putting greens, up to which point the British players were equally good. We were very poor by comparison, although quite equal to the recognised two putts per green standard. I consider that we can never hope to beat the Americans unless we learn to putt. This lesson should be taken to heart by British golfers.'

Britain, in fact, won the first two matches on home soil, at Moortown in 1929 and Southport and Ainsdale in 1933, but the pattern of American dominance had been set and Ray's words would ring true for decades to come. It is only in recent times that the Americans have been beaten regularly, causing them to turn the same complaint against themselves.

There were some memorable moments to come, such as the

victory of Dai Rees's team at Lindrick in 1957 and the tied match at Royal Birkdale in 1969. In a famous gesture of sportsmanship, Jack Nicklaus conceded Tony Jacklin's final three-foot putt with the words, 'I'm sure you would have holed it but I was not prepared to see you miss.' Earlier, as they had walked off the 18th tee, Nicklaus had asked Jacklin, that summer's Open champion, how he felt. 'Bloody awful,' came the reply. 'I thought you might,' Nicklaus said. 'If it's any consolation, so do I. A bugger isn't it?'

In 1977, Nicklaus made a crucial intervention when he wrote to Lord Derby, the president of the Professional Golfer's Association, and suggested that golfers from the continent of Europe be brought into the match to improve the level of competition. It did not help much in 1979 and certainly not in 1981 at Walton Heath, when the Americans turned up with their strongest ever side. All but Bruce Lietzke were, or went on to become, Major champions. The result of the match was never in doubt and the Americans won 18^1/$_2$–9^1/$_2$.

That match was the first in which Jacklin had not been involved since his debut in 1967. For the 1983 match, Jacklin was appointed captain and he wanted to make changes. 'We'd been second-class to the Americans for too long, and I don't mean because we were always losing, but in the manner in which our side operated and in which our players were treated,' he said. In came Concorde, cashmere, caddies and confidence. Jacklin wanted the team to travel in style, look stylish and, for the first time, to take their own caddies. In the process, he instilled a layer of confidence that had previously been lacking.

Europe, as they were now, lost again at Palm Beach Gardens that year but it was a thrilling match in which the Americans sneaked home by a point. Seve Ballesteros, whom Jacklin anointed as his general on the course, walked into the team room at the end and cajoled everyone into celebrating. They had come within a whisker of victory, and he was sure it would be theirs in two years' time.

The inspirational Spaniard was right. At the Belfry in 1985, Europe won for the first time in twenty-eight years. This was the first of seven victories in eleven matches, with one tied. Two years later at Muirfield Village, in an even more famous victory, America lost on home soil for the first time. A quintet of golfers, all born within a year of each other, formed the backbone of the upsurge in European golf, and they were perhaps all at their peak – Seve, Nick Faldo, Bernhard Langer, Sandy Lyle and Ian Woosnam – while Jose Maria Olazabal was emerging as a new Spanish genius.

Langer showed remarkable resilience to recover from missing a putt at Kiawah Island in 1991, which meant America regained the Ryder Cup. The contest had gone down to the final putt on the final hole of the final match. Tom Watson led the USA to victory again at the Belfry two years later but then Bernard Gallacher, at Oak Hill in 1995, and Ballesteros, on home soil at Valderrama in 1997, returned the Cup to Europe. Brookline, in Boston, hosted an acrimonious match in 1999, the home side making the biggest ever final-day comeback, from 4 points down, to win. There were reports of rudeness to the visiting players by the crowd, and the home players and caddies wildly celebrated a magnificent putt from Justin Leonard on the 17th green when Olazabal was still to play.

Captains Sam Torrance and Curtis Strange did much to restore proper etiquette after the 2001 match at the Belfry was postponed for a year due to terrorist atrocities. Torrance led his team to victory, and then Langer took a team with no Major champions to Oakland Hills and came away with a record 9-point win. It could not happen again, it was thought, but at the K Club in Ireland in 2006, Woosnam's squad did exactly the same, playing golf that was breathtaking in quality and conviction.

What would Samuel Ryder have made of the 2006 match? He would no doubt have been astonished at many aspects of it, the sheer scale, the infrastructure and security requirements, the fact that the biggest international sporting event ever staged in Ireland netted the host country around €130 million. He may have been shocked at the size of the gallery, around 45,000 each day, and their raucousness, but he would have approved of their fair-mindedness.

Most importantly, he would have been thrilled at the spirit displayed by the players on each team, competitive, yet friendly and respectful. Ryder once said of his creation, 'I have done several things in my life for the benefit of my fellow men but I am certain I have never done a happier thing than this. I look upon the Royal and Ancient game as being a powerful moral force that influences the best things in humanity. I trust the effect of this match will be to influence a cordial, friendly and peaceful feeling throughout the whole civilised world.'

RYDER CUP RESULTS 1927–2006

Year	Venue	USA	EUROPE
2006	K Club, County Kildare, Ireland	9 1/2	18 1/2
2004	Oakland Hills CC, Bloomfield Township, Michigan	9 1/2	18 1/2
2002	The Belfry, Sutton Coldfield, England	12 1/2	15 1/2
1999	The Country Club, Brookline, Massachusetts	14 1/2	13 1/2
1997	Valderrama GC, Sotogrande, Spain	13 1/2	14 1/2
1995	Oak Hill CC, Rochester, New York	13 1/2	14 1/2
1993	The Belfry, Sutton Coldfield, England	15	13
1991	The Ocean Course, Kiawah Island, South Carolina	14 1/2	13 1/2
1989	The Belfry, Sutton Coldfield, England	14	14
1987	Muirfield Village GC, Dublin, Ohio	13	15
1985	The Belfry, Sutton Coldfield, England	11 1/2	16 1/2
1983	PGA National GC, Palm Beach Gardens, Florida	14 1/2	13 1/2
1981	Walton Heath GC, Surrey, England	18 1/2	9 1/2
1979	The Greenbrier, West Virginia	17	11
1977	Royal Lytham and St Annes, England	12 1/2	7 1/2
1975	Laurel Valley GC, Ligonier, Pennsylvania	21	11
1973	Muirfield, Scotland	19	13
1971	Old Warson CC, St Louis, Missouri	18 1/2	13 1/2
1969	Royal Birkdale GC, Southport, England	16	16
1967	Champions GC, Houston, Texas	23 1/2	8 1/2
1965	Royal Birkdale GC, Southport, England	19 1/2	12 1/2
1963	East Lake CC, Atlanta, Georgia	23	9
1961	Royal Lytham and St Annes, England	14 1/2	9 1/2
1959	Eldorado CC, Palm Desert, California	8 1/2	3 1/2
1957	Lindrick GC, Yorkshire, England	4 1/2	7 1/2
1955	Thunderbird CC, Palm Springs, California	8	4
1953	Wentworth GC, Wentworth, England	6 1/2	5 1/2
1951	Pinehurst CC, Pinehurst, North Carolina	9 1/2	2 1/2
1949	Ganton GC, Scarborough, England	7	5
1947	Portland Golf Club, Portland, Oregon	11	1
1937	Southport and Ainsdale GC, England	8	4
1935	Ridgewood CC, Ridgewood, New Jersey	9	3
1933	Southport and Ainsdale GC, England	5 1/2	6 1/2
1931	Scioto CC, Columbus, Ohio	9	3
1929	Moortown GC, Leeds, England	5	7
1927	Worcester CC, Worcester, Massachusetts	9 1/2	2 1/2

It all began for me at Valderrama.

12 | FROM VALDERRAMA TO OAKLAND HILLS 1997–2004

I turned professional before I had the chance to play in the Walker Cup. By the time I came along, it wouldn't have made that much difference, whereas previously it used to help you get invitations into certain tournaments. It didn't really affect me. I wanted to be a professional and that was it.

You don't aspire to play in the Ryder Cup, it's just one of those things that happens if you play well enough, but when you get a taste of one competition, you don't want to miss it again.

My first taste of it was, to say the least, different. Seve Ballesteros was captain in Spain. He did things his way and we won, but I didn't play as much as I would have liked, bearing in mind that I had qualified second for the team.

In Brookline, Mark 'Jessie' James was fantastic. His dry wit and humour entertained us throughout the week and we played really well, unbelievably at times. Perhaps we got a bit ahead of ourselves when we went into the last day 4 points ahead and, yes, we did lose, but what people tend to forget is that the Americans on the final day played golf that was nothing less than stunning. That's been overlooked. They played sensational golf and deserved to win, given how they had come back when their backs were to the wall.

What happened on the 17th, when some of their players ran on to the green, was unfortunate, but sometimes emotions run very high. Justin Leonard holed a fantastic putt and I'm sure those people who invaded wish they hadn't. I don't hold it against them. It was a very disappointing day to come away losing, but when you lose to better golf you have to hold your hand up and admit it.

From what I've read, the Americans who went away from the K Club held their hands up and admitted that they were outplayed. That's the way it should be. On that Sunday at Brookline we were outplayed. That is a fact.

At the Belfry in 2002, Sam Torrance took the reins, and he's another who wears his heart on his sleeve. He was fantastic and got the best out of his players. He did have a great bunch, but he had to get them to play and he did. It was, for us, a really special win, given what Sam and the Belfry have shared through the years. We all want to win for our captains but for Sam, the hero of 1985 when he'd holed the winning putt there, it was so very special.

Detroit under Bernhard Langer was different in that he is not as extrovert as some of our captains have been, but he was thorough. He is very straight down the line, and he has his way of doing things. You have the utmost respect for him because of his record as a player. He's a double Major winner and those are few and far between – particularly these days, in the era of Tiger. Bernhard made some great decisions that week and his behind the ropes team was outstanding. Thomas Bjorn was one of his lieutenants and I'm sure he helped a great deal and was hugely influential, and that's to take nothing away from Bernhard.

It was a record win for us over there. We were very comfortable, but not so comfortable as we were at the K Club, although we did know we had a very good team. What we've done this past couple of times is respond in the correct way to the ebb and flow of match-play golf. When the momentum has started going against us, we've been able to nick it back at the last minute. If you can do that, it carries you through, but if you get the wrong side of things like that, it's hard to come back, and that's what's happened to the Americans.

For the life of me, I have no idea why the Americans in the last six or seven Ryder Cups have not gelled as a team as well as we have. Tiger's indifferent record in the tournament is strange because he is far and away the best player in the world. You would think, too, when they come from a land where, at college level, everything is team, team, team, they would embrace the team spirit even more than we do. I honestly don't know why they don't. They are all fantastic players as individuals.

As for the future, I've got one Ryder Cup left in me for sure, and maybe two or three. After that, I would love to be Ryder Cup captain. I'd like to think that I'd do a pretty decent job and it would be an honour to be given the chance.

I certainly learned a lot from the captains at the K Club. Woosie kept everything plain and simple for us and had twelve players on top of their form. I owe him a great debt of gratitude for having the bottle to pick me. I hope I repaid him with the points he wanted from me, but he was simply Captain Fantastic.

For America, Tom appeared to do everything absolutely right, both before and during the match. He was everything that you could have wanted from a captain, but on this occasion he just came up against a team who played out of their socks. He was very gracious in defeat and exceptionally kind to me throughout.

I will remember the lessons I learned from both of them if I ever get the chance to follow in their spikes.

1997: VALDERRAMA GOLF CLUB, Sotogrande, Spain

	EUROPE		UNITED STATES
FOURSOMES – morning			
J.M. Olazabal and C. Rocca (1 hole)	1	0	D. Love III and P. Mickelson
N. Faldo and L. Westwood	0	1	F. Couples and B. Faxon (1 hole)
J. Parnevik and P.U. Johansson (1 hole)	1	0	T. Lehman and J. Furyk
C. Montgomerie and B. Langer	0	1	T. Woods and M. O'Meara (3 and 2)
FOURBALLS – afternoon			
C. Rocca and J.M. Olazabal	0	1	S. Hoch and L. Janzen (1 hole)
B. Langer and C. Montgomerie (5 and 3)	1	0	M. O'Meara and T. Woods
N. Faldo and L. Westwood (3 and 2)	1	0	J. Leonard and J. Maggert
J. Parnevik and I. Garrido (halved)	1/2	1/2	T. Lehman and P. Mickelson (halved)
FOURSOMES – morning			
C. Montgomerie and D. Clarke (1 hole)	1	0	F. Couples and D. Love III
I. Woosnam and T. Bjorn (2 and 1)	1	0	J. Leonard and B. Faxon
N. Faldo and L. Westwood (2 and 1)	1	0	T. Woods and M. O'Meara
J.M. Olazabal and I. Garrido (halved)	1/2	1/2	P. Mickelson and T. Lehman (halved)
FOURBALLS – afternoon			
C. Montgomerie and B. Langer (1 hole)	1	0	L. Janzen and J. Furyk
N. Faldo and L. Westwood	0	1	S. Hoch and J. Maggert (2 & 1)
J. Parnevik and I. Garrido (halved)	1/2	1/2	J. Leonard and T. Woods (halved)
J.M. Olazabal and C. Rocca (5 and 4)	1	0	D. Love III and F. Couples
SINGLES			
I. Woosnam	0	1	F. Couples (8 and 7)
P.U. Johansson (3 and 2)	1	0	D. Love III
C. Rocca (4 and 2)	1	0	T. Woods
T. Bjorn (halved)	1/2	1/2	J. Leonard (halved)
D. Clarke	0	1	P. Mickelson (2 and 1)
J. Parnevik	0	1	M. O'Meara (5 and 4)
J.M. Olazabal	0	1	L. Janzen (1 hole)
B. Langer (2 and 1)	1	0	B. Faxon
L. Westwood	0	1	J. Maggert (3 and 2)
C. Montgomerie (halved)	1/2	1/2	S. Hoch (halved)
N. Faldo	0	1	J. Furyk (3 and 2)
I. Garrido	0	1	T. Lehman (7 and 6)
	14¹/₂	**13¹/₂**	

Victorious captain – **Seve Ballesteros**

1999: THE COUNTRY CLUB, Brookline, Boston, Massachussetts

EUROPE			UNITED STATES
FOURSOMES – morning			
P. Lawrie and C. Montgomerie (3 and 2)	1	0	D. Duval and P. Mickelson
S. Garcia and J. Parnevik (2 and 1)	1	0	T. Lehman and T. Woods
M.A. Jimenez and P. Harrington (halved)	1/2	1/2	D. Love III and P. Stewart (halved)
D. Clarke and L. Westwood	0	1	J. Maggert and H. Sutton (3 and 2)
FOURBALLS – afternoon			
C. Montgomerie and P. Lawrie (halved)	1/2	1/2	J. Leonard and D. Love III (halved)
S. Garcia and J. Parnevik (1 hole)	1	0	J. Furyk and P. Mickelson
M.A. Jimenez and J.M. Olazabal (2 and 1)	1	0	J. Maggert and H. Sutton
D. Clarke and L. Westwood (1 hole)	1	0	D. Duval and T. Woods
FOURSOMES – morning			
P. Lawrie and C. Montgomerie	0	1	J. Maggert and H. Sutton (1 hole)
D. Clarke and L. Westwood (3 and 2)	1	0	J. Furyk and M. O'Meara
M.A. Jimenez and P. Harrington	0	1	S. Pate and T. Woods (1 hole)
S. Garcia and J. Parnevik (3 and 2)	1	0	J. Leonard and P. Stewart
FOURBALLS – afternoon			
D. Clarke and L. Westwood	0	1	P. Mickelson and T. Lehman (2 and 1)
S. Garcia and J. Parnevik (halved)	1/2	1/2	D. Love III and D. Duval (halved)
M.A. Jimenez and J.M. Olazabal (halved)	1/2	1/2	J. Leonard and H. Sutton (halved)
P. Lawrie and C. Montgomerie (2 and 1)	1	0	S. Pate and T. Woods
SINGLES			
L. Westwood	0	1	T. Lehman (3 and 2)
D. Clarke	0	1	H. Sutton (4 and 2)
J. Sandelin	0	1	P. Mickelson (4 and 3)
J. Van de Velde	0	1	D. Love III (6 and 5)
A. Coltart	0	1	T. Woods (3 and 2)
J. Parnevik	0	1	D. Duval (5 and 4)
P. Harrington (1 hole)	1	0	M. O'Meara
M.A. Jimenez	0	1	S. Pate (2 and 1)
J.M. Olazabal (halved)	1/2	1/2	J. Leonard (halved)
C. Montgomerie (1 hole)	1	0	P. Stewart
S. Garcia	0	1	J. Furyk (4 and 3)
P. Lawrie (4 and 3)	1	0	J. Maggert
	13 1/2	**14 1/2**	

Victorious captain – **Ben Crenshaw**

2002: THE BELFRY GOLF and COUNTRY CLUB, Sutton Coldfield, West Midlands

	EUROPE		UNITED STATES
FOURBALLS – morning			
D. Clarke and I. Bjorn (1 hole)	1	0	T. Woods and P. Azinger
S. Garcia and L. Westwood (4 and 3)	1	0	D. Duval and D. Love III
C. Montgomerie and B. Langer (4 and 3)	1	0	S. Hoch and J. Furyk
P. Harrington and N. Fasth	0	1	P. Mickelson and D. Toms (1 hole)
FOURSOMES – afternoon			
D. Clarke and T. Bjorn	0	1	H. Sutton and S. Verplank (2 and 1)
S. Garcia and L. Westwood (2 and 1)	1	0	T. Woods and M. Calcavecchia
C. Montgomerie and B. Langer (halved)	1/2	1/2	P. Mickelson and D. Toms (halved)
P. Harrington and P. McGinley	0	1	S. Cink and J. Furyk (3 and 2)
FOURSOMES – morning			
P. Fulke and P. Price	0	1	P. Mickelson and D. Toms (2 and 1)
S. Garcia and L. Westwood (2 and 1)	1	0	J. Furyk and S. Cink
C. Montgomerie and B. Langer (1 hole)	1	0	S. Verplank and S. Hoch
D. Clarke and T. Bjorn	0	1	T. Woods and D. Love III (4 and 3)
FOURBALLS – afternoon			
N. Fasth and J. Parnevik	0	1	M. Calcavecchia and D. Duval (1 hole)
C. Montgomerie and P. Harrington (2 and 1)	1	0	P. Mickelson and D. Toms
S. Garcia and L. Westwood	0	1	T. Woods and D. Love III (1 hole)
D. Clarke and P. McGinley (halved)	1/2	1/2	S. Hoch and J. Furyk (halved)
SINGLES			
C. Montgomerie (5 and 4)	1	0	S. Hoch
S. Garcia	0	1	D. Toms (1 hole)
D. Clarke (halved)	1/2	1/2	D. Duval (halved)
B. Langer (4 and 3)	1	0	H. Sutton
P. Harrington (5 and 4)	1	0	M. Calcavecchia
T. Bjorn (2 and 1)	1	0	S. Cink
L. Westwood	0	1	S. Verplank (2 and 1)
N. Fasth (halved)	1/2	1/2	P. Azinger (halved)
P. McGinley (halved)	1/2	1/2	J. Furyk (halved)
P. Fulke (halved)	1/2	1/2	D. Love III (halved)
P. Price (3 and 2)	1	0	P. Mickelson
J. Parnevik (halved)	1/2	1/2	T. Woods (halved)
	15½	**12½**	

Victorious captain – **Sam Torrance**

189

2004: OAKLAND HILLS COUNTRY CLUB, Bloomfield Township, Michigan

	EUROPE	UNITED STATES	
FOURBALLS – morning			
C. Montgomerie and P. Harrington (2 and 1)	1	0	P. Mickelson and T. Woods
D. Clarke and M.A. Jimenez (5 and 4)	1	0	D. Love III and C. Campbell
P. McGinley and L. Donald (halved)	1/2	1/2	C. Riley and S. Cink (halved)
S. Garcia and L. Westwood (5 and 3)	1	0	D. Toms and J. Furyk
FOURSOMES – afternoon			
M.A. Jimenez and T. Levet	0	1	C. DiMarco and J. Haas (3 and 2)
C. Montgomerie and P. Harrington (4 and 2)	1	0	D. Love III and F. Funk
D. Clarke and L. Westwood (1 hole)	1	0	T. Woods and P. Mickelson
S. Garcia and L. Donald (2 and 1)	1	0	K. Perry and S. Cink
FOURBALLS – morning			
S. Garcia and L. Westwood (halved)	1/2	1/2	J. Haas and C.DiMarco (halved)
D. Clarke and I. Poulter	0	1	T. Woods and C. Riley (4 and 3)
P. Casey and D. Howell (1 hole)	1	0	J. Furyk and C. Campbell
C. Montgomerie and P. Harrington	0	1	S. Cink and D. Love III (3 and 2)
FOURSOMES – afternoon			
D. Clarke and L. Westwood (5 and 4)	1	0	J. Haas and C. DiMarco
M.A. Jimenez and T. Levet	0	1	P. Mickelson and D. Toms (4 and 3)
S. Garcia and L. Donald (1 hole)	1	0	J. Furyk and F. Funk
P. Harrington and P. McGinley (4 and 3)	1	0	T. Woods and D. Love III
SINGLES – Sunday			
P. Casey	0	1	T. Woods (3 and 2)
S. Garcia (3 and 2)	1	0	P. Mickelson
D. Clarke (halved)	1/2	1/2	D. Love III (halved)
D. Howell	0	1	J. Furyk (6 and 4)
L. Westwood (1 hole)	1	0	K. Perry
C. Montgomerie (1 hole)	1	0	D. Toms
L. Donald	0	1	C. Campbell (5 and 3)
M.A. Jimenez	0	1	C. DiMarco (1 hole)
T. Levet (1 hole)	1	0	F. Funk
I. Poulter (3 and 2)	1	0	C. Riley
P. Harrington (1 hole)	1	0	J. Haas
P. McGinley (3 and 2)	1	0	S. Cink
	181/2	**9**1/2	

Victorious captain – **Bernhard Langer**